THE BLAZED TRAIL/Outdoor Diary

THE BLAZED TRAIL/Outdoor Diary

PREFACE

"Heaven is under our feet as well as over our heads."
Henry David Thoreau, WALDEN

The purpose of this book is to make your outdoor experiences both meaningful and rewarding. It's everything you'll need to know, and want to remember—from the moment you decide on your vacation to the many memories of years to come.

The Outdoor Diary is the how, when, where and why of a great vacation. From FISHING through ENRICHING YOUR OUTDOOR EXPERIENCES you'll find descriptions of more than 100 trips, treks, excursions, and outdoor activities. Whether you're planning a month, a week, or a day, there's something in this book for you. It also contains suggestions on what to do, where to stay, and how much to spend.

Most important, this book does much more than help you plan a vacation, it helps you plan *your* vacation. There are Personal Information and Trip PLANer sections to organize *every* detail of your vacation. And a Personal Diary along with a Photo Album to help remember it.

In short, your Outdoor Diary is a planner, a guide, a permanent ready reference—to be used and enjoyed now and in the years ahead. It comes to you exclusively from Abercrombie & Fitch, and is dedicated to all who agree that Heaven is under their feet.

TABLE OF CONTENTS

Preface *page 5*

Personal Information *page 8*
Outdoor Diary **&**
Photo Album *pages 9-37*
Three-year Calendar *page 38*
The Sportsman's Prayer *page 39*

Fishing *page 40*
Trout and Salmon *page 42*
Salt Water Game Fish *page 56*
Exotics *page 71*
In Addition *page 75*

Hunting *page 86*
Upland Shooting *page 88*
Water Fowl *page 92*
Big Game *page 95*
On Firearms *page 105*

The Outdoor Adventure *page 108*
Trips and treks in Africa,
Iceland, Greenland, Alaska, Peru,
Galapagos, Brazil and Nepal

Woods & Waters *page 126*
Underwater *page 128*
Climbing *page 132*
Canoeing *page 133*
Family Outings *page 136*
Start Them Young *page 140*

Courts & Courses *page 144*
Tennis *page 146*
Golf *page 148*
Skiing *page 151*
Sailing *page 154*

Enriching Your Outdoor Experience *page 158*
Outdoor Observations *page 160*
Capturing Your Experience on Film *page 162*
Choosing and Using Binoculars *page 167*
Conservation Organizations *page 170*

Planning Your Outdoor Year *page 174*
A&F TRIP PLANner *page 176*
Recollections *page 178*
Outdoor Travel Specialists *page 188*
It's Your Book Now *page 188*

Index *page 189*
Acknowledgements/Photo Credits *page 191*

PERSONAL INFORMATION

Name

Company Name

Address

Residence

Tel.

Other

FINANCIAL

Checking Account No.

Bank Name

Address

Official's Name   Tel.

Other

Passport No.

Date of Issue

Place of Issue

Expires

Social Security No.

AUTOMOBILE

Auto No.

Registration No.   Expires

License No.

Auto Insurance Policy No.

Carrier's Name

Agent's Name

Tel. No.

HEALTH

In case of emergency notify   Immunizations

Physician's Name   Tel.

Address

Health Insurance Policy No.   Blood type

Carrier's Name   Allergies

Agent's Name   Tel.

CREDIT CARDS	Company	Card No.	Expires	Notify in case of loss

	Name	Address	Telephone Number
Attorney			
Dentist			

Outdoor Diary

The following 28 pages are for memories photographed and written. For the greatest flexibility we've intentionally omitted the standard diary format and instead divided it into five sections, each separated by a page for your photos.

The sections and ruled lines are suggestions only. When you wish to make an entry, you can either use or ignore them.

This diary was designed for you. Your thoughts. Your memories. We hope you will use and enjoy it often.

_____   _____

_____   _____

_____   _____

_____   _____

_____   _____

_____   _____

_____   _____

_____   _____

_____   _____

_____   _____

_____   _____

_____   _____

_____   _____

Spring
The streams and lakes have freed themselves
And run and shout like youngsters out from school.
My rod is new. My flies are freshly tied.
Each cast I make is sure to raise a fish.
Or, if no fish should rise, I cast, as sure again.
                    R.A. Brown 1962

_____ _____

_____ _____

_____ _____

_____ _____

_____

_____ _____

_____ _____

_____ _____

_____ _____

_____ _____

_____ _____

_____ _____

Summer

Streams are now quiet, lakes are calm.
My dry fly floats for minutes between casts.
The fish I take are larger than in Spring,
But come to net more easily, it seems.
A couple of the windings of my rod are frayed.
R.A. Brown 1962

Autumn
There's little time to fish this year.
The streams run low. Red leaves float on the lake.
I get few fish, but treasure every strike.
Mornings are cold, sunset too soon.
A fringe or ice appears along the shore.
                    R.A. Brown 1962

Winter

The angler's year has gone.
Ice covers all the waters that I fished.
I feel its chill within myself.
Yet Spring will come, the streams and lakes released,
And I shall fish again—somewhere.
                    R.A. Brown 1962

1976

JANUARY	FEBRUARY	MARCH	APRIL	MAY	JUNE
S M T W T F S	S M T W T F S	S M T W T F S	S M T W T F S	S M T W T F S	S M T W T F S
1 2 3	1 2 3 4 5 6 7	1 2 3 4 5 6	1 2 3	1	1 2 3 4 5
4 5 6 7 8 9 10	8 9 10 11 12 13 14	7 8 9 10 11 12 13	4 5 6 7 8 9 10	2 3 4 5 6 7 8	6 7 8 9 10 11 12
11 12 13 14 15 16 17	15 16 17 18 19 20 21	14 15 16 17 18 19 20	11 12 13 14 15 16 17	9 10 11 12 13 14 15	13 14 15 16 17 18 19
18 19 20 21 22 23 24	22 23 24 25 26 27 28	21 22 23 24 25 26 27	18 19 20 21 22 23 24	16 17 18 19 20 21 22	20 21 22 23 24 25 26
25 26 27 28 29 30 31	29	28 29 30 31	25 26 27 28 29 30	23 24 25 26 27 28 29	27 28 29 30
				30 31	

JULY	AUGUST	SEPTEMBER	OCTOBER	NOVEMBER	DECEMBER
S M T W T F S	S M T W T F S	S M T W T F S	S M T W T F S	S M T W T F S	S M T W T F S
1 2 3	1 2 3 4 5 6 7	1 2 3 4	1 2	1 2 3 4 5 6	1 2 3 4
4 5 6 7 8 9 10	8 9 10 11 12 13 14	5 6 7 8 9 10 11	3 4 5 6 7 8 9	7 8 9 10 11 12 13	5 6 7 8 9 10 11
11 12 13 14 15 16 17	15 16 17 18 19 20 21	12 13 14 15 16 17 18	10 11 12 13 14 15 16	14 15 16 17 18 19 20	12 13 14 15 16 17 18
18 19 20 21 22 23 24	22 23 24 25 26 27 28	19 20 21 22 23 24 25	17 18 19 20 21 22 23	21 22 23 24 25 26 27	19 20 21 22 23 24 25
25 26 27 28 29 30 31	29 30 31	26 27 28 29 30	24 25 26 27 28 29 30	28 29 30	26 27 28 29 30 31
			31		

1977

JANUARY	FEBRUARY	MARCH	APRIL	MAY	JUNE
S M T W T F S	S M T W T F S	S M T W T F S	S M T W T F S	S M T W T F S	S M T W T F S
1	1 2 3 4 5	1 2 3 4 5	1 2	1 2 3 4 5 6 7	1 2 3 4
2 3 4 5 6 7 8	6 7 8 9 10 11 12	6 7 8 9 10 11 12	3 4 5 6 7 8 9	8 9 10 11 12 13 14	5 6 7 8 9 10 11
9 10 11 12 13 14 15	13 14 15 16 17 18 19	13 14 15 16 17 18 19	10 11 12 13 14 15 16	15 16 17 18 19 20 21	12 13 14 15 16 17 18
16 17 18 19 20 21 22	20 21 22 23 24 25 26	20 21 22 23 24 25 26	17 18 19 20 21 22 23	22 23 24 25 26 27 28	19 20 21 22 23 24 25
23 24 25 26 27 28 29	27 28	27 28 29 30 31	24 25 26 27 28 29 30	29 30 31	26 27 28 29 30
30 31					

JULY	AUGUST	SEPTEMBER	OCTOBER	NOVEMBER	DECEMBER
S M T W T F S	S M T W T F S	S M T W T F S	S M T W T F S	S M T W T F S	S M T W T F S
1 2	1 2 3 4 5 6	1 2 3	1	1 2 3 4 5	1 2 3
3 4 5 6 7 8 9	7 8 9 10 11 12 13	4 5 6 7 8 9 10	2 3 4 5 6 7 8	6 7 8 9 10 11 12	4 5 6 7 8 9 10
10 11 12 13 14 15 16	14 15 16 17 18 19 20	11 12 13 14 15 16 17	9 10 11 12 13 14 15	13 14 15 16 17 18 19	11 12 13 14 15 16 17
17 18 19 20 21 22 23	21 22 23 24 25 26 27	18 19 20 21 22 23 24	16 17 18 19 20 21 22	20 21 22 23 24 25 26	18 19 20 21 22 23 24
24 25 26 27 28 29 30	28 29 30 31	25 26 27 28 29 30	23 24 25 26 27 28 29	27 28 29 30	25 26 27 28 29 30 31
31			30 31		

1978

JANUARY	FEBRUARY	MARCH	APRIL	MAY	JUNE
S M T W T F S	S M T W T F S	S M T W T F S	S M T W T F S	S M T W T F S	S M T W T F S
1 2 3 4 5 6 7	1 2 3 4	1 2 3 4	1	1 2 3 4 5 6	1 2 3
8 9 10 11 12 13 14	5 6 7 8 9 10 11	5 6 7 8 9 10 11	2 3 4 5 6 7 8	7 8 9 10 11 12 13	4 5 6 7 8 9 10
15 16 17 18 19 20 21	12 13 14 15 16 17 18	12 13 14 15 16 17 18	9 10 11 12 13 14 15	14 15 16 17 18 19 20	11 12 13 14 15 16 17
22 23 24 25 26 27 28	19 20 21 22 23 24 25	19 20 21 22 23 24 25	16 17 18 19 20 21 22	21 22 23 24 25 26 27	18 19 20 21 22 23 24
29 30 31	26 27 28	26 27 28 29 30 31	23 24 25 26 27 28 29	28 29 30 31	25 26 27 28 29 30
			30 31		

JULY	AUGUST	SEPTEMBER	OCTOBER	NOVEMBER	DECEMBER
S M T W T F S	S M T W T F S	S M T W T F S	S M T W T F S	S M T W T F S	S M T W T F S
1	1 2 3 4 5	1 2	1 2 3 4 5 6 7	1 2 3 4	1 2
2 3 4 5 6 7 8	6 7 8 9 10 11 12	3 4 5 6 7 8 9	8 9 10 11 12 13 14	5 6 7 8 9 10 11	3 4 5 6 7 8 9
9 10 11 12 13 14 15	13 14 15 16 17 18 19	10 11 12 13 14 15 16	15 16 17 18 19 20 21	12 13 14 15 16 17 18	10 11 12 13 14 15 16
16 17 18 19 20 21 22	20 21 22 23 24 25 26	17 18 19 20 21 22 23	22 23 24 25 26 27 28	19 20 21 22 23 24 25	17 18 19 20 21 22 23
23 24 25 26 27 28 29	27 28 29 30 31	24 25 26 27 28 29 30	29 30 31	26 27 28 29 30	24 25 26 27 28 29 30
30 31					31

The Sportsman's Prayer

Live in Peace and Harmony with Nature—be not in Conflict with her, for her beauty and her pleasures are many.

Poison not her waters, for they are the home of our fishes, and the drink of our game, as well as ourselves.

Poison not her atmosphere, for it is the source of her life, and it is necessary for our continued well being.

Foul not with litter, her woods, her meadows, her mountains, nor her waters, for they provide us with beauty and the rich gifts of her bounty.

Take not more fish from her seas, nor her lakes, nor her streams than we can use at one time, so that there will be more tomorrow.

Take not the life of her beasts wantonly, nor of her fowl, for it is wrong, and you shall be condemned by your fellow Sportsmen.

Disturb not her young, nor their homes, so that they may go forth and they may multiply.

Tread lightly on her paths, lest they be damaged—walk gently across her meadows, lest they be covered with scars which will not heal.

Pluck not the wild flowers from her bosom, nor the fragile plants from her mountains, lest they be rare and pass away forever, to be no more.

Abuse not her laws, nor her generosity, lest her gifts be withheld from your sons and your daughters, and your grandsons and your granddaughters, forever.

Gene Bushnell

FISHING

Trout and Salmon
Mistassini Park, Quebec
Montana's Legendary Rivers
Cumilahue River, Chile
Patagonia, Argentina
Browns & Rainbows in New Zealand
Four Rivers, Iceland
Three Beats, Scotland
Great Northern Fishing Camps, Labrador
George River Lodge, Quebec

Salt Water Game Fish
Tropic Star Lodge, Panama
Punta Carnero, Ecuador
Casa Mar, Costa Rica
Parismina Tarpon Rancho, Costa Rica
Pez Maya, Yucatan
Deep Water Cay Club, Bahamas
Walker's Cay, Bahamas
Light Tackle in Bermuda
Club Pacifico, Panama

Exotics
Dorado in Paraguay and Argentina
El Dorado Lodge, Colombia

In Addition
Europe on Business?—Pack A Rod!
National Fish Stamp Program
Plan Your Trip Carefully
Improving Your Technique
Preparing and Packing Your Fishing Tackle
Preserving Your Trophy
It Can Happen to Anyone
An Ounce of Prevention

Trout and Salmon

MISTASSINI PARK, QUEBEC

Looking down from the small float plane, you can see almost as much water as land, a product of the receding glaciers of the last Ice Age. The Pepeshquasati, along with the Cheno, Toqueco, Temiscamie, and several smaller rivers, funnel into the head of 110-mile long Lake Mistassini and its 80-mile long sister, Lake Albanel. These lakes are in the heart of Quebec's Mistassini Park, an expanse of some 5,200 square miles of virgin wilderness lying above the 50th parallel. The famed

Rupert River starts its journey to James Bay from the flank of Lake Mistassini. The Broadback and Eastmain plot their destinies nearby, also emptying into James Bay.

This is brook trout country; the breeding grounds of a famous native species that was originally found only in Eastern North America. Brook trout fishing is good in June, but it is best the last week of August and the first two weeks of September when the spawning runs start up many of the rivers. If you're after trophy brookies, the place to be is in one of the satellite camps right on one of the spawning rivers.

Vieux Poste Lodge is located on a small island near the northern end of Lake Mistassini. It is the jumping off point for the short flights into the satellite camps. At Vieux Poste, you sleep in comfortable cottages with cold running water. Showers and toilet facilities are located separately.

The bush camps usually accommodate four to six anglers and they are tent camps. They are not fancy, but they are close to some of the finest brook trout fishing and that's the important consideration. Food at the bush camps is prepared by the guides and it is wholesome and plentiful. Fishing is done both from motorized canoes and by wading. At this time of year, the rivers are restricted to fly fishing only.

How To Get There

You can fly all the way to Vieux Poste with the final hop made by float plane from Lake Cache at the southern end of Lake Mistassini. If you prefer driving, you can drive to within a dozen miles of Vieux Poste to Temiscamie Base and then fly over from there.

What to Take

You are above the 50th parallel and the weather varies. It can be quite warm during mid-summer, but you should be prepared for cool temperatures. Toward late August and in early September, the days are often warm, but the nights and mornings are cold. The weather changes rapidly. You could have snow flurries or just

Lake trout, Canada

plain snow by early September.

If you plan to fish the special brook trout run, you'll need flyrods and streamer patterns of flies. Floating lines would be the prime choice, but it would be worthwhile taking a sink tip line and possibly a sinking line for those deeper pools.

There are plenty of fish in Lake Mistassini and Lake Albanel. You can catch lake trout during mid-season by trolling deep, but the lakers are closer to the surface during June and September. There are always small lake trout in the mouth of the Albanel River and you can take these on light spinning tackle. Northern pike run big in this country and spinning or plug gear is ideal. You can handle most pike on 10-pound-test line or less if you have had some fishing experience, but if you're a newcomer, you might want to go to 12-pound-test or possibly 15-pound-test. Dardevles in red and white, five of diamonds, and the potato bug pattern are as good as anything for northerns. You can also take them on fly and the best patterns are large streamers with plenty of shiny Mylar in the wings.

Cost

Mistassini Park and its lodges are controlled by the Quebec Government. Rates are reasonable and they are fixed. The best advice is to book early for the special brook trout season, because accommodations at Vieux Poste and the satellite camps is limited.

For further information contact:
*Quebec Ministry of Tourism,
Fish, and Game
12 St. Anne's Street
Quebec, Quebec, Canada*

MONTANA'S LEGENDARY TROUT STREAMS

Most trout fisherman across the country yearn for a trip to Montana's famous trout waters and, once they have visited that magnificent big sky country, they hunger for the day when they can return. Streams such as the Yellowstone, Madison, Gallatin, Boulder, Big Hole, Firehole, and the Snake are household words among fly fishermen.

Although fishermen sometimes argue the merits of one stream against another, Montana fly fishing pioneer Dan Bailey is the first to tell you that it is more important *when* you come than where you fish. Any stream is good if you are there at the right time, but unfishable if you don't time your arrival perfectly. In other parts of the trout world, May and June are excellent months, yet in Montana, most trout fishing doesn't begin until July (and sometimes mid July). Once the streams do become fishable, the season will continue through October.

The Firehole, Henry's Fork of the Snake, and some of the smaller spring creeks seem to clear earlier in the year and may be fishable from early June. Of course, the salmon fly hatch is famous if you can time it right. On some streams it begins as early as the first week in June and may not occur until mid-July on other streams. If you want to fish this hatch, it's a matter of telephoning Dan Bailey, Will Godfrey, or other fishing headquarters before you journey to Montana. When they tell you to

come, that's the time to board a plane and get out there quickly.

What To Take

Life in Montana is casual and comfortable. Your clothing selection should follow the same guidelines. It could get cool, especially in the evenings or early morning, so warm clothes are advisable. At the same time, you should have a few lightweight shirts and trousers for those warm days. Felt soled or cleated waders are a must for the big waters of the West, and a rain jacket to slip on in case of a shower is also a basic requirement.

Fishing the wider Western rivers dictates longer rods. It's not a question of being able to handle the fish, because any flyrod will hold a trout once hooked. You will have to cast greater distances and you will be casting larger, more wind-resistant flies. That doesn't mean you have to leave your shorter and lighter flyrods at home, but you should be equipped to handle the longer casting assignments first.

An 8½ or 9-foot flyrod is a good choice for big streamer flies and you can handle most dry fly fishing with an 8-footer. There are times your standard trout tackle will also work and it pays to bring all the combinations you can. Reels, of course, should be armed with at least 50 yards of backing and preferably 100 yards. You'll be using floating flylines most of the time, but don't forget a sink tip and a fast sinking line. You should be prepared to handle any option. Weight forward flylines are the number one choice, but double tapers are effective if a particularly delicate presentation is required.

Everyone talks about the big Western fly patterns, but it's a good idea to take your fly boxes of the smaller Eastern patterns with you. If you don't have the larger flies, they are available from the excellent tackle shops in the area. You'll need dry flies, nymphs, some wet flies, and streamers and bucktails.

Guides

Guiding services are available from all of the tackle shops in the region. The cost of a guide ranges from $65 to $75 per day for two anglers. It is not absolutely necessary to have a guide and most tackle shops in this part of the world are delighted to help anyone catch fish. They'll tell you where to fish, what to use, and do their best to help you have a good time.

For further information contact:

Dan Bailey
Dan Bailey Fly Shop
P.O. Box 1019
Livingston, Montana 59047
Telephone: 406-222-1673

Will Godfrey
Will's Fly Fishing Center
P.O. Box 68
Island Park, Idaho 83429
Telephone: 208-558-9960

Bud Lilly
Bud Lilly Trout Shop
Box 387
West Yellowstone, Montana 59758
Telephone: 406-646-7801

Bob Jacklin
Bob Jacklin's Fly Shop
Box 604
West Yellowstone, Montana 59758
Telephone: 406-646-7336

CUMILAHUE RIVER, CHILE

It's only fishable for eight of its fifteen miles, but Chile's Cumilahue River is possibly one of the ten best trout streams in the world. Unlike most rivers in the Chilean Lake Region, the Cumilahue is a meandering stream with unbelieveably clear water and it is wadable throughout its fishable length.

Unless you've been to this part of the trout fisherman's world, you may not realize that most fishing is done from boats that are floated down the wide, fast-flowing rivers that pour out of the Andes and cascade downward to the sea or connect the chain of lakes. Finding wadable rivers with big trout, a tremendous quantity of fish, and an impressive food supply is unusual.

Tales of the fishing in this part of the world become somewhat magnified by the time they filter back to North America. There are huge trout in Chile and there are small trout in Chile. You will probably catch some of both, but don't expect trophy trout on every cast. It just doesn't happen that way.

On the Cumilahue, the season begins on October 15th and runs through March 31st. The river is high in October and the water temperature is right at 48 or 49 degrees. At this time of year, you will catch both brown trout and rainbows and you stand the best chance of getting big fish. Rainbows will reach six pounds or better and the browns may go as large as a dozen pounds.

One reason for the superb growth of this native fish is the presence of the pancora, a small crab-like crustacean that is exceptionally abundant and provides the mainstay of the diet. Insect life on most streams is poor because they are too fast flowing. On the Cumilahue, insect life is rich with plenty of caddis, stonefly, and mayfly nymphs.

By late November or early December, you can dry fly fish on the Cumilahue. The first hatches are mayflies, with both yellow and brown caddis flies appearing in December. Dries dressed on a number 12 hook will do well. By the end of December, a big, sulphur-colored mayfly appears and hatches take place in the evening. You can imitate this pattern with any big dry fly tied on a number 8 or 6 hook or even larger.

To fish the Cumilahue effectively, you should have a full range of fly patterns that includes nymphs, wet flies, wooly worms, small and large streamers, and a variety of dry flies.

Even during the middle of the summer, the river remains reasonably cold with temperatures in the low to mid 50's. Perhaps in February (the equivalent of August in the Northern Hemisphere) the river may reach 60 degrees. On January 7, 1973, the Cumilahue gave up the largest brown trout on record, a 21½ pounder taken from the Rock Pool on the lower river. During the course of a season, a half-dozen ten pounders may be taken, a couple dozen six pounders, but many, many fish in the four to six-pound-class will be hooked. You can expect a

Cumilahue River, Chile

pair of felt-soled waders and preferably two just as insurance against unrepairable leaks. A wading staff is worthwhile, but you won't need a net, because Adrian insists on releasing almost every trout (except for one or two trophies you may want to have mounted).

To fish the Cumilahue properly, you'll need at least two flyrods. The first should be capable of handling a number 8 weight—forward flyline and the second rod should be balanced with a five-weight-line. You can bring other fly outfits, but you should have these two. In the spring, much of the fishing is done with sinking lines, but the floater comes into play and can be used throughout the season. Again, it's a good idea to have a sink tip or two with you for nymph fishing and for working streamers or wet flies.

It might be necessary to follow a big fish downstream, but you don't need an excessive amount of backing on your flyreels. The same tackle you use back home will work in Chile on the Cumilahue. Early in the season, you can use 0X and 1X leaders with streamers. As the water gets clearer, you may go as light as 4X, 5X, and even 6X.

There are very few insects at streamside and you won't be bothered by them. The one exception is in January when there is a hatch of a large horsefly called a tabano that will bite. That's the time to have insect repellent handy. It helps.

Cost

The standard rate at the

minimum of one fish over three pounds on any given day.

Accommodations

Adrian and Pat Dufflocq operate the Cumilahue Fishing Lodge on the banks of the Cumilahue near Llifen, Chile. Adrian is perhaps Chile's best fly fisherman and an accomplished angler by any standards in the world. He knows and loves the trout fishing in his land, speaks perfect English, and can tell you stories of big fish that will cause your blood to race.

The lodge is nestled among beds of bright flowers in an Andean valley and the beauty of the scene defies written description. There are five bedrooms with double beds,

accommodating eight to ten anglers. Each room has its own private bath. The meals are a delightful blend of Chilean dishes and universal foods prepared by Pat Dufflocq. The rustic interior of the lodge with its huge fireplace and beautiful wooden floors is a haven for any trout fisherman. Laundry is done daily at no charge to the guests and each meal is an opportunity to sample another variety of the famous Chilean wines.

What To Take

Although arrangements can be made if you prefer to fish one of the other rivers from a boat, the Cumilahue is fished strictly by wading. You'll need at least one

Cumilahue Fishing Lodge is $33 per day, which includes lodging, food, wine, laundry, and other incidentals. There is a charge of $20 per day for a boatman or a gillie to carry your gear at streamside if you so desire. It is not necessary to have a guide or a gillie. Should you want to engage the services of Adrian (which is a worthwhile experience), the cost is $30 for one person, $25 each for two people, and $20 each for three or four fishermen.

For further information contact:

(October 15 through March 31st)
Adrian Dufflocq
Cumilahue
Llifen, Chile

(April 1st to October 1st)
Adrian Dufflocq
P.O. Box 14138
Santiago, Chile

Lake Region, Argentina

PATAGONIA, ARGENTINA

Some of the finest and most exciting trout fishing in the world is found in southern Argentina. San Carlos de Bariloche, a city some 850 air miles south of Buenos Aires, forms the hub of the trout area and, coincidentally, the first planting of trout from North American hatcheries took place here some 70 years ago.

Browns and rainbows are the two principal species, but there are also brook trout and landlocked salmon. Argentina produces very large trout, but, like Chile, there are also smaller fish. It's not uncommon to take fish weighing six or seven pounds or more, but you can also have a lot of fun with two, three, and four pound fish.

The season in Argentina begins in November and runs to April 15th. Since the seasons are reversed from those in the Northern Hemisphere, you must remember that the rivers are high in November and early December from the spring runoff. They start to drop by mid-December and improve daily throughout January and February. March marks the beginning of fall and the days are warm and calm, but the nights start to become cool.

Fishing with Douglas Reid

Douglas Reid, grandson of the late Guy Dawson who helped to pioneer fishing in Patagonia, is perhaps the best fishing guide in Argentina. Your headquarters for this trip will be at the Hotel Los Andes in the village of San Martin de los Andes in the Province of Neuquen. San Martin is about 125 miles north of Bariloche and in the heart of one of the best fishing areas. From San Martin, you will fish a radius of 75 miles or more depending on water conditions and your own personal preferences.

Fishing is done from boats and also by wading. You often have a choice of either lake fishing, stream fishing, or a bit of both.

Lake fishing is good almost all season long, but it is best during the first two months. The streams, on the other hand, get better later in the season when the high waters characteristic of springtime anywhere have had a change to subside.

It can be windy in Argentina with

breezes filtering down the valleys from the lofty Andes. For that reason, at least one of your flyrods should be a 9 footer with a weight-forward line. You'll find a fast-sinking line as valuable as a floater, especially if you fish the river mouths and the lakes. Lake fishing can either be trolling or casting.

Fly patterns are a matter of choice, but you should carry some large streamers and bucktails with you. In fact, don't overlook some of the husky saltwater patterns, but make sure you have a rod and line weight that can handle these bulkier flies.

Being in this beautiful part of Argentina is a lifetime experience. The mountains are magnificent, the rivers swift flowing, forests are swathed in green, and there are flowers everywhere. On the other hand, deluxe hotel facilities do not exist in this part of Argentina. Hotels and inns are clean and the food is fine, but one shouldn't expect gourmet dishes. Like most fishing spots in the world, the food is plain, but plentiful.

The cost of seven days fishing is $1,120 for one person: $1,470 for two fishermen. These prices include hotel accommodations and meals, transportation to and from Bariloche, boats, and guides.

You can obtain further information or book the trip through:
Adventures Unlimited
19 East 45th Street
New York, New York 10017
Telephone: 212-682-3600
or
Adventures Unlimited
220 Post Street
San Francisco, California (94108)
Telephone: 415-397-2300

A Unique Trout Experience

The southern part of Argentina is one of the last frontiers for large trout. As one travels southward beyond Bariloche toward Tierra del Fuego, the Andes become more massive and the wilderness areas more pronounced. This is rugged country with beautiful rivers and sparkling lakes—waters that don't receive much fishing pressure simply because they are hard to reach.

If you're willing to live in tents and journey by car below Bariloche, there's a unique experience in store. Wenckheim Safaris, Box 484, Bariloche, Argentina, specializes in guiding anglers to virgin waters in the Province of Santa Cruz. Where you fish will depend on the time you select and your personal preferences, but this area has produced many large brook trout up to 8 pounds as well as trophy browns and rainbows.

The usual trip takes ten days from Bariloche and the cost is approximately $1,000 per person for two anglers. There is a modest reduction per person if three or four anglers make the trip. These are custom-tailored trips and they should produce some of the best trout fishing you have ever experienced.

If you would like to know more about this safari, write directly to Wenckheim Safaris in Argentina or you may contact the Braniff Outdoor Council, Braniff International, Exchange Park, Dallas, Texas.

Brown trout, New Zealand

BROWNS AND RAINBOWS IN NEW ZEALAND

No discussion of premier trout waters would be complete without some mention of New Zealand. There are many who consider the trout fishing on these two islands for browns and rainbows to be the finest in the entire world (with no exceptions). Since brown trout were originally introduced from Britain in 1867 and rainbows from California's Russian River sixteen years later, the quality of fishing in New Zealand has been unsurpassed.

These fish thrived because of the abundance of natural food, a virgin environment of cold, clear lakes and flowing rivers, and gravel bottom streams that present ideal spawning conditions. Not only did they multiply, but they soon developed a strain that was unique for its size and fighting qualities. It's interesting to note that New Zealanders have developed their own system of determining the condition of a trout by comparing its size to its weight.

The country is divided into the North Island and the South Island. North Island is smaller, slightly warmer, and offers better rainbow trout fishing. South Island stretches some 550 miles in length with a width of perhaps 120 miles. It has more mountains than North Island and there are seventeen peaks reaching more than 10,000 feet.

Perhaps the best known trout fishing takes place in the lake systems of the central North Island. What angler in the world hasn't heard of Lake Rotorua or Lake Taupo and the Tongariro River. This is rainbow trout paradise with the fish in Rotorua averaging almost three pounds and those in Taupo over four pounds. Rainbows that weigh in double figures are taken from both areas. There are also plenty of brown trout, but they are outnumbered by the rainbows and most of the big ones are taken after dark.

In Lake Taupo, for example, the summer months of December, January, and February are best for fly fishing around the mouths of rivers that empty into the lake. At other times, fish can be taken on fly in the lake. The most effective patterns are streamers that resemble a smelt and both floating and sinking lines should be on

hand to work the fish either shallow or deep.

Although North Island has received more publicity in recent years because of the superb rainbow fishing, South Island is just gaining notoriety as a haven for brown trout. Over the years, some of the best catches of consistently large brown trout have come from South Island streams and lakes, yet little publicity was forthcoming.

This is dry fly country and you can do exceptionally well in most of the rivers with a variety of dries. The best season is December through April and many rivers are designated as fly fishing only streams.

In South Westland, for example, sea-run brown trout average five pounds and run as high as eleven pounds. There are also big rainbow trout all over the island and these fish are in top fighting condition.

If you do decide to plan a trip to New Zealand, you should allow at least two weeks to sample the fishing and a month would be even better. You would want to spend a minimum of a week on North Island and another week on South Island. There is travel time in between, so it works out to perhaps five days of fishing on each island if you allow two weeks.

Keep in mind that peak seasons vary depending on where you fish. The northern tip of North Island is almost semi-tropical, while it stays cool at the southern tip of South Island. You can readily see why seasonal differences are commonplace. However, the point to remember is that you can trout

fish most of the year somewhere in New Zealand and it should rank among the best trout fishing you've ever experienced. It would be difficult to find a visiting angler who didn't dream of the day he could return and "really get to do some serious fishing"

A wealth of information is available from the:
New Zealand Government Travel Commissioner, 630 Fifth Avenue, New York, New York 10020

FOUR RIVERS IN ICELAND

A combination of sensible fishery management and good fortune have vaulted Iceland into the number one position as the best place in the world for Atlantic salmon fishing. Unlike the North American salmon, Icelandic fish do not winter off Greenland and have not been subjected to the indiscriminate netting that has so drastically depleted stocks on this side of the Atlantic. The feeding grounds of Iceland's salmon population remain a mystery, known only to the fish themselves.

Equally important, sophisticated fishery management began in Iceland before the turn of the century when that country first banned the open ocean netting of salmon in its territorial waters. Since then, careful control of the river fishing, a restocking program operated under the watchful eye of the country's Institute of Fresh Water Fisheries, and an enlightened attitude of the river owners themselves, have contributed to the maintenance and improvement of Iceland's salmon population. In the past decade alone, Iceland's annual production of salmon has nearly doubled.

Iceland lies in the Atlantic just below the Arctic Circle, about halfway between New York and Moscow. It boasts slightly less than 30,000 square miles and only 205,000 residents, most of whom live along the coast. Almost half of them live in or near the capital city of Reykjavik.

The coastline is marked by deep fjords and a substantial tidal range. Inland, mountain ranges poke skyward to a height of 9,000 feet. The landscape is virtually treeless, but there are rich green pasturelands in a picturesque setting against the deeper browns of the lava beds.

Iceland's climate is relatively mild along the coast and is influenced by an extension of the Gulf Stream. During the summer, average temperatures are in the 50's and 60's, but the weather is extremely changeable. You should come prepared for rain, wind, and cold that will disappear as suddenly as it appeared. When you pack your clothing, consider that a day can start off windless and warm with a clear blue sky. Before you finish fishing, the sky may be overcast and the countryside misty or covered with a sea fog. A biting wind can drive rain in your face and it will be cold. Yet, this is the type of weather when the salmon hit best and rain means that the fish will continue to move upriver. If you have a down jacket and a rain suit, you'll stay comfortable in spite of the elements.

Tackle To Take and Some Fishing Tips

The preferred method of fishing for Atlantic salmon anywhere in the world is with a flyrod and artificial flies. In Iceland, spinning and even bait fishing is permitted on many rivers, but some of the rivers leased to Americans are being offered to clients on a fly fishing only basis.

Selecting tackle is somewhat of a personal thing, but there are some general guidelines. Depending on the river you fish and even varying

by each pool, you will be fishing different conditions. Your skill with a flyrod will help you determine what to use, but you would be well advised to bring at least two flyrods and possibly more.

One rod should be capable of handling a number 9-weight-forward line and it would probably be 8½ or 9-feet long. Rods handling heavier lines also have a place, as do shorter and lighter rods. There are times when you will have to make long casts and there are times when the wind will

Atlantic salmon, Iceland

blow and casting will be difficult. Some anglers have used 9-foot flyrods that handle a 10 weight line and others have used lines as heavy as a number 11. These were special situations in a strong wind, but we add this information so that you can properly prepare. On the other side of the coin, you can use featherweight rods with balanced lines if you enjoy that phase of the sport.

Reels should be of the salmon variety or large enough to hold a flyline along with 150 yards of backing. There are some pools where it's tough to follow a fish downstream—at least not very quickly and you don't want to run out of backing.

A good pair of waders with felt soles is important and you may want to take an extra pair along just in case. You should also consider a wading staff. It's not necessary, but it is sometimes nice to have when the water is swift and cold.

Fly patterns are a matter of personal choice. You'll find the universal salmon patterns in use such as the Blue Charm, Jock Scott, Black Doctor, Silver Gray, and others. In addition, there are patterns that are Icelandic in design and they are very effective as well as an interesting addition to your collection. Any salmon fisherman knows he has to be prepared for a variety of water conditions and it's no different in Iceland. Flies dressed on number 4, 6, and 8 hooks are popular, but you should have a variety both larger and smaller.

To be ready for any eventuality, you should have at least three types of flylines on interchangeable spools or pre-looped so that they can be changed quickly. Obviously, a floating flyline is the prime choice, but a sinking line can be equally important. And, the new sink tips in which the first ten feet sink and the rest of the line floats can prove invaluable.

Every fisherman has his own theories about what flies to use when, and Icelandic experts are no different. They suggest that you use larger patterns when water temperatures are low and smaller patterns as the temperatures rise. Small flies are a better choice for quiet waters, while larger flies seem to raise more fish in faster water. If the water is colored, you can try a larger fly, but when it is clear, start with smaller offerings. Bright fish just in from the sea seem to show a preference for one of the shrimp patterns and also for brighter flies in general. On the other hand, fish that have been in the river for a while will rise to a smaller fly.

Understanding The System

Icelandic law regulates salmon fishing and all rivers are open on June 15th and close on September 15th. A 12-hour fishing day is permitted and it is usually broken into two sections. The first session is from 7 a.m. to 1 p.m., and fishing begins again at 4 p.m. and continues to 10 p.m. There may be variations on some rivers, but it all adds up to 12 hours a day.

Each fishing lodge is provided with a log book and every salmon caught (even if released) must be recorded in that book. The purpose of this log is to provide statistical information and each entry is tailored to tell a great deal about each fish. You'll probably enjoy leafing through this log in your free hours.

Icelanders are extremely friendly people and they are immaculate housekeepers. Many of the inns and lodges are rustic and all are quite comfortable. There is a rough tackle room outside the main lodge where each angler is expected to leave his fishing tackle, waders, and heavy or wet clothing. You'll find that a pair of slippers or moccasins will come in handy.

Twelve hours of fishing is a long day and the rule in most lodges is one of reserve and quiet, because fisherman could be catching up on their sleep at any time. Meals are served before you go fishing and when you return from fishing. Since fishing is over at 10 p.m. on most rivers, dinner can be as late as 10:30 or 11:00. It's a long day for everyone and your host would appreciate your having dinner as soon after you come off the stream as possible.

The Laxa i Aldaldal

The Laxa i Aldaldal basks in the reputation of the Queen of Iceland's salmon rivers. This river is located on the northwestern shore of Iceland and flows northward. Fishing is done by wading, from the bank, or from a boat in two pools. The river has a long tradition and remains unique because its fish average about double the size of those in any other Icelandic river. Laxa fish average a dozen pounds or more.

Although the fish arrive off the north coast by early June and are in the river by the opening of the season, the best time is after the first week of July through most of August.

Only seven fishermen can fish the beats on this stretch of river and the lodge is right on the river. The food is excellent and served in true Scandanavian tradition, and the custom is to serve four meals a day.

Costs average about $2,000 per rod/week with transfers to and from Reykjavik. Since it is perhaps the finest salmon beat in Iceland, bookings should be made well in advance.

The Grimsa

Lying in the beautiful Borgarfjordur district just three hours by car from Reykjavik, the Grimsa flows southwest from its lake source to its mouth in the Hvita, a large glacial river. The Hvita enters the sea a few miles downstream at Borganes, an historic town first mentioned in literature in "Egil's Saga" in the 13th century.

The upper waters of the Grimsa flow gently through pleasant meadowlands, but the river speeds up and assumes a more dramatic character downstream with intermittent waterfalls and rapids. An unobstructed gravel bottom without the characteristic lava outcroppings common to most Icelandic rivers makes wading easy and permits lighter tackle to be used.

There's a new lodge on the Grimsa designed by salmon fisherman and architect Ernest Schwiebert. The lodge is perched on a rocky promontory overlooking the Laxfoss where the casual observer can watch salmon jumping the falls through picture windows.

Grimsa salmon arrive in early June and start upriver. They gather at the base of Laxfoss until the falls lower after the spring runoff and then leap the falls to continue their journey upstream. Prime season begins the second week of July and runs through the third week of August.

The rate throughout the season is approximately $2,000 including transfers from and back to Reykjavik.

Midfjardara River

The Midfjardara is situated on the north coast of Iceland about 45 minutes by plane or 4½ hours by car from Reykjavik. It has always been known as one of the best rivers in Iceland for salmon, holding a large stock of fish that average 8 or 9 pounds. This is above the normal average for most rivers and there are a number of Midfjardara fish that reach 20 pounds.

The river is born 47 miles inland and flows to the sea. Through its length, there are some 80 pools and runs that hold salmon and they are available to visiting anglers. Guides are available to transport anglers to the pools and to render assistance during the day.

A comfortable fishing lodge is situated along the river and there is a bedroom assigned to each rod. Typical of the region, there are four meals each day. Meals are wholesome, filling, and delicious

The Laxa In Skogarstrond

The Laxa River in Skogarstrond is located on the west coast of Iceland about 3 hours drive from Reykjavik. Compared to other fine river in Iceland, it is relatively small, extending only about four miles. Salmon only travel a distance of two miles and then their journey is blocked by a waterfall.

Its small size makes it easy to fish and it holds plenty of salmon in the 8 to 17 pound range. There are no notable cliffs and the river is not very wide. The banks are low and slope gently, yet there are about 15 pools and runs to fish. It's an easy river to learn to fish by yourself, yet river guidance is available. A small lodge with two bedrooms, a living room, kitchenette, and bath is situated right on the river.

Since fishing rights on these and the other Icelandic rivers are auctioned off annually, information on the current leasee can be obtained directly from Adventures Unlimited or write
Ideal Fishing
Austurstraeti 6
Reykjavik, Iceland

THREE BEATS IN SCOTLAND

Ballathie Beat
River Tay

The Ballathie Beat on the River Tay extends for 1½ miles and is really divided into two beats with alternate fishing. This is a big river and most fishing is done from a boat, but bank fishing from either side is also effective. During periods of extremely low water, wading is possible.

Anglers have the option of either fly tackle or spinning gear (if they so desire). Although the season opens in mid-January and fish are taken consistently until the season closes in mid-October, statistics for the past five years demonstrate that at least 75% of the salmon were caught in August, September, and the first two weeks of October.

The Tay produces big fish with an average weight over 11 pounds and, last year, there were 109 fish taken over 20 pounds. All fishing is under the personal supervision of Mr. John Bennett. The beat is limited to six rods and accommodations are arranged at the beautiful Ballathie House Hotel at Stanley (near Perth). This is an exquisite country house with large bedrooms and private bathrooms. Meals are excellent and include a choice of wines during dinner.

Prices vary with the week as they do on all salmon waters. During the prime time, the charges are a little over $1,000 per rod and the price includes meals, accommodations, ghillies, boats,

Salmon flies

tranfers to and from the hotel to the airport, and the loan of fishing tackle and waders if necessary.

Anglers may fish rods of their choice, but Mr. Bennett recommends long flyrods and plenty of backing on the reel. This is a big river and the fish are husky. Spinning tackle should be tailored to handle 12 or 15-pound-test lines.

Taymount Beat
River Tay

Located just below the Ballathie Beat, the Taymount Beat offers another 1½ miles of premier fishing water on the famed River Tay. There are actually two beats and they are fished alternately just as on the Ballathie Beat. It is all good water with excellent fly fishing runs. Most fishing is done from a boat, but bank fishing and some wading is available.

You are again under the personal supervision of Mr. John Bennett and are transported to the beat by car. Access is easy and excellent. The Taymount Beat is limited to five rods and accommodations are at the Ballathie House Hotel.

In the past five seasons, this beat yielded 1,750 salmon with an average weight of almost 14 pounds. The cost per rod is approximately $700 and includes meals, hotel, and the other services provided on the Ballathie Beat.

Tulchan Beat
River Spey

There are four beats on this prime fishing water and it is rather exclusively devoted to fly fishing,

although spinning tackle is permitted. The Spey is another wide river and perhaps the most famous in Scotland for salmon fishing. In addition, the river is equally known for its fine sea trout fishing.

This angling is mostly wading and chest waders are a decided advantage. Waders are available if you don't have your own, but it's always more comfortable to use your own personal waders if you have room to pack them.

The four beats are fished alternately and each is 1¼ miles long with good access and fishing from both banks. From mid-April until the end of September, fishing for salmon is excellent on these beats. The records for the past five years emphasize that one month is as good as the next. Salmon tend to average about 10 pounds, while the seatrout average almost 3 pounds.

Accommodations are available for five rods and guests will stay at the Tulchan Lodge, a stately Scottish country house on the 21-thousand-acre Tulchan Estate, eight miles from Grantown-on-Spey. There are double bedrooms with private bath for guests, and Cordon Bleu cooks provide international menus or local dishes to order. The Spey is only a short walk from the front door.

General Information

Scotland offers memorable salmon fishing for visiting anglers from January through November. The seasons vary on the different rivers, but there is generally some fishing in progress at any time of the year except December.

The climate in Scotland is cool with temperatures often in the low 40's, reaching the mid-50's or possibly 60 degrees in the summer. There are warmer days, but you should be prepared for lower temperatures.

If you would like to learn more about salmon fishing in Scotland, contact Adventures Unlimited.

GREAT NORTHERN FISHING CAMPS, LABRADOR

With 120,000 square miles of wilderness and 4900 miles of coastline, Labrador forms the most northern part of North America on the Eastern Seaboard. The coast is sparsely settled with small fishing villages and the interior is virtually unmarked by man. There are no roads and no railroads in Labrador. To reach Goose Bay, you must fly in (except during the summer when steamer service is available).

Until recently, this idyllic land of lakes and rivers was virtually inaccessible to the visiting sportsman because of lack of camps and facilities. Ever so slowly, pioneering outfitters like Norm Hathaway are establishing tiny camps on virgin waters. Norm is an expert American angler who has spent the past 20 years developing fishing opportunities in Labrador. The season is short, extending from July to September and accommodations are extremely limited in capacity, so it's wise to book early.

Atlantic Salmon and Brook Trout

Labrador's Eagle River struggles for 150 miles until it empties into Sandwich Bay. The river is located southeast of Goose Bay and the only way to reach it is by charter aircraft. Norm Hathaway maintains his Eagle River Camp on one of the best Atlantic salmon stretches. Unlike other rivers, you don't have to worry about perfect timing or expect to find only grilse. A steady run of bright salmon begins during the last of July and continues right through August.

The Eagle is a wild river and fishing is restricted to a flyrod only. Atlantic salmon have been averaging ten pounds or better and there are big brook trout everywhere. The problem is to sneak a fly past the three and four pounders to get to the trophy fish. Each season, a number of squaretails in the seven to eight pound range are landed at Eagle River Camp. Fishing is done by wading and also from boats.

Accommodations

The small, but comfortable camp on Eagle River boasts permanent buildings of log, plywood, and cedar shake with gas heaters and gas lighting. Bath facilities are indoors and there is plenty of hot water. Flush toilets add to your comfort in the middle of the wilderness. Good beds with firm mattresses add to your sleeping comfort. Meals are served family style in the cookhouse dining area and are well-prepared by full-time cooks. If you leave the table hungry, it's your own fault.

What to Take

Labrador is a long way north and, although you may encounter warm temperatures, it can also be quite cool (especially late in the season). Take warm clothing in case it gets colder than you expect and bring a rainsuit. You should have warm socks and warm underwear, but pack some light shirts and trousers along with wool and cotton flannel.

You'll need a pair of waders or hipboots for wading and a pair of light shoes plus warmer boots (low type) for the boats. Fly fishing only is the rule at Eagle River. You should have a minimum of two flyrods including an 8½ footer that can handle an 8 or 9 weight flyline. Long casts are not necessary from the boat, but they may be while wading.

Remember that the salmon average over 10 pounds and that means they will take plenty of line when hooked. The reels you select should handle a minimum of 100 yards of 15 or 20-pound-test backing plus a flyline, and 150 yards of backing is preferable. Your basic flyline should be a floater, but consider one of the new sink tips as a second line and

possibly a high density sinking line as a third option. That will enable you to fish every level.

Standard salmon fly patterns will work and you'll also enjoy using some of the patterns that Norm Hathaway developed up there. They are available at the camp to supplement your normal complement of patterns.

Cost

A week at Eagle River Camp is $685 including the flight from Goose Bay to camp and back. The price includes guides, boats, licenses, and the preparation of fish to take home if you so desire.

Snegamook Lake Lodge

Snegamook Lake lies about an hour's flying time northwest of Goose Bay. Here, you will find outstanding fishing for ouananiche (landlocked salmon), lake trout, and northern pike. The lake also contains an unbelieveable number of small brook trout in the one to two pound class. During the first two weeks of September, you can combine the fishing with excellent wingshooting for Canada geese.

Norm Hathaway maintains a Cessna 180 on floats at the camp and for a nominal flying rate of $50 per hour, he can put you on nearby lakes that boast brook trout from four to seven pounds. You also have the option of flying out to lakes that hold Arctic char in the five to fifteen pound range.

What To Take

Clothing requirements are identical to those for the Eagle River Camp. If you prefer fly fishing, you should have a pair of flyrods with at least one of them in the 8½ to 9-foot range. Reels should have plenty of backing and you would be wise to consider floating, sink tip, and fast sinking flylines. Fly patterns should include various streamer flies such as marabous, Silver Doctors, Gray Ghosts, Mickey Finns, and even some salt water patterns. The latter will not only work on big brook trout, but they can be very effective on husky northern pike.

You might want to include a spinning rod or two and perhaps a bait casting outfit. Line tests should be between 8 and 15 pounds for pike fishing. Ouananiche and big brookies can be handled on light or ultra-light spinning rods.

Cost

The price at Snegamook is $625 per week, Goose Bay to Goose Bay.

For more information contact your travel agent, or Fish and Game Frontiers, Pearce Mill Road, Wexford, Pa. 15090 Tel. 412-935-1577 or write
Norm Hathaway
Great Northern Fishing Camps
P.O. Box 143
Brewer, Maine

GEORGE RIVER LODGE, QUEBEC

With its headwaters in Lake Michikamau, the George River is the largest river flowing into Ungava Bay in Northern Quebec. The prime fishing is for Atlantic salmon, but there is also excellent sport for brook trout and Arctic char. This is fly fishing country and the George River Lodge only allows ten rods for salmon.

The season is relatively short because you are so far north. It begins in early July and continues through September. In the early fall, you have the option of combining caribou hunting with salmon fishing. The main run of salmon seems to work its way up the George in August and early September.

Accommodations

Guests are housed in oil-heated cabins and there is electric power for refrigerators and coolers. The food is wholesome, plentiful, and delicious. One guide is assigned for two fishermen and canoes with outboards are included in the rates. Fishing and hunting permits are extra and can be purchased at camp.

What To Take

On the George River, you're above the 56th parallel and the days are cool with plenty of rain during the summer. You will need warm clothing and a good rainsuit. Like other places in the far north, insects can be a problem and you should be equipped with plenty of repellent. In addition, clothing that can be secured at neck and wrists will make life more comfortable.

The camp supplies headnets if necessary.

A good pair of felt-soled waders are important and you should also take a pair of well broken-in walking boots. Don't forget your sunglasses, because the sun does shine on the George River.

Your primary salmon flyrod should be 8½ or 9-feet long, but you might want to take a lighter flyrod or two for brook trout. A typical salmon reel with 150 yards of backing is also a wide choice. Salmon flies should be dressed on number 4, 6, and 8 hooks and most of the standard patterns will work well. The Blue Charm, Thunder and Lightning, Silver Gray, Silver Doctor, Jock Scott, and others all take fish.

Flies on 8, 10, or 12 hooks are ideal for brook trout and you can use streamers or bucktails as well. In fact, it doesn't hurt to pack a few larger streamers just in case.

How To Get There

The easiest way is to fly Quebecair from Montreal to Schefferville and then by charter aircraft to the George River Lodge.

Cost

Like most salmon camps, rates vary by the week in the season. It costs more for the weeks when more salmon are in the river. You can figure it will cost between $750 and $1,000 or more per week.

For further information contact *Adventures Unlimited*

Salt Water Game Fish

TROPIC STAR LODGE, PANAMA

Pinas Reef surges sharply upward from the floor of the Pacific Ocean a few miles offshore and 150 miles southeast of Panama City. This underwater plateau is pressured by ocean currents and has become a virtual fishbowl, with species after species congregating and feeding in this concentrated area. Heading the list is the impressive black marlin, one of the great gladiators of the Indo-Pacific and prized adversary among big game anglers.

It was the abundance of black marlin in the waters off Pinas Bay that tempted the late Ray Smith into building the luxurious Tropic Star Lodge. Before the Lodge was literally hacked out of the dense Darien Jungle, anglers had to charter a boat in Balboa and make the long trip past the Perlas Islands almost to the Colombian border.

Black marlin are as plentiful over Pinas Reef as any other known hotspot in the world today. Perhaps the only place to rival this fishing is Cairns, Australia where the average size of the marlin may be larger, but it is questionable whether there are more fish. The important consideration is that Tropic Star is a short flight from Miami or New Orleans and that any angler stands a good chance of landing a black marlin in this hemisphere.

Seasonally, blacks have been taken at any time of the year, but the best season is from December

Roosterfish, Panama

to April. Right around Christmas and New Year's when the rainy season is over, the marlin seem to appear in particularly large numbers, but there is never a guarantee. You'll find, however, that more marlin are caught early in the morning and again late in the afternoon than during the middle of the day. Marlin fishing seems to be better on an outgoing tide.

Although black marlin have been the big attraction at Tropic Star Lodge, there are enough other species in residence to keep most anglers busy all year long. Striped marlin are taken regularly and there are terrific runs of sailfish. It's difficult to pinpoint the times of these major sailfish runs (some have taken place in January and others in March and April), but when they happen, you can't release them fast enough.

The majority of anglers at Pinas Bay concentrate on trolling for big fish and they miss out on the fun of light tackle sport with casting gear. You can cast to a variety of species over the reef from the scrappy bonito (on which the marlin feed) to dolphin and even sailfish. Inshore, there is another world waiting to be explored and you can tangle with snapper, roosterfish, jacks, African pompano, and a hundred other species.

In fact, the Lodge has obtained a couple of 23 foot Sea Crafts for the light tackle inshore and offshore fishing. The other boats are twin-engine, 31 foot Bertrams. Boat crews are experienced in big game fishing and there are several crews who are well-versed in light tackle techniques. However, it's a good idea to let the Lodge know in advance if you plan to light tackle fish. They will gladly assign crews experienced in this sport.

What To Take

The boats at Tropic Star are equipped with big game tackle for marlin fishing. Most of this gear is 80-pound-class, but a few 50-pound outfits are available. There is a $20 rental charge per week for the use of this tackle. Keep in mind, however, that it is difficult for anyone to keep tackle in top shape when it is used by a different angler each week. For that reason, it's a good idea to bring your own if you have it. You'll be more comfortable using tackle with which you are familiar and you'll know it is in prime condition

If you are interested in trying for a world record or catching fish on light tackle, it is imperative that you bring your own. Thirty-pound-test class tackle or lighter will have to be your own. And, if you intend to do some casting with fly, spinning, or plug gear, you must bring the tackle with you along with all the lures you think you will need.

The Lodge also imposes a charge of $2.50 for each cable leader used by an angler. You have the option, of course, of bringing your own hooks and leaders.

Accommodations

The Darien Jungle may be the densest in the world, but don't let that fool you. Tropic Star Lodge is a luxurious resort that is well-maintained and where service to the guest is emphasized. All of the rooms are air-conditioned and they are extremely spacious with equally large private baths. The lawns are manicured and the flowers are always striking.

The dining room and bar are separated by a few steps and a partition. From your table, you can look out over Pinas Bay and the cuisine is excellent. Great care is taken in the preparation of the food and in the serving. If you gain weight, don't say we didn't warn you.

Known in Spanish as "El Palacio", the late Ray Smith built his own private residence atop a hill overlooking the bay. It can accommodate six people with three huge bedrooms, each with private bath and dressing room. It is available at extra cost.

Dress at Tropic Star is informal. Lightweight fishing clothes are in order throughout the day, but in the evening, the women usually wear light dresses or slacks and the gentlemen go to dinner in sports shirts and slacks. Ties are never worn.

Cost

The basic cost of one week at Tropic Star Lodge is $1,185 per person, two fishermen to a boat. This includes the charter flight to and from Panama City, room, meals, boat, crew, and bait. Bar bills are extra and there is the $20 charge for rented tackle. The standard week is from Saturday to Saturday and there is no fishing on the day of arrival because that has been set aside for boat maintenance.

For more information contact:

Tropic Star Lodge, S.A.
374 Kingston Crescent
Winnipeg, Manitoba, Canada
R2M OT8
Telephone: 204-453-5947

or write direct to

Tropic Star Lodge of Panama, S.A.
Apartodo 6813
Panama City 5
Republic of Panama

PUNTA CARNERO, ECUADOR

It's the perfect spot for striped marlin and other blue water gamefish. Less than a dozen miles off Salinas, Ecuador, the mighty Humboldt Current sweeps northward, carrying a river of cool water that started down in the Antarctic. Just north of this point, the Humboldt turns westward and sets out across the Pacific. To balance things, there is a warm current that moves southward and also turns west when it brushes against the Humboldt. Known as the Panama or Counter Equatorial Current, this body of warmer water brings other species south with it to the area around Salinas.

When you fish these impressive waters, you are at a gamefish junction. Striped marlin tend to follow the edge of the Humboldt northward, feeding on baitfish that have collected. Baitfish congregate because the current causes an upwelling of nutrients from the deep that bloom when they reach the warmer surface waters. The baitfish feed on plankton and the marlin feast on the baitfish.

It is not uncommon to sight 60 to 100 striped marlin in a given day. There are times when stripes are scarce, but you can generally count on seeing a few and baiting a good percentage of them. Almost all the marlin are spotted cruising on the surface first and then the boat is maneuvered for the intercept. It's exciting to watch a skipping balao slip in front of a marlin and then thrill to the marlin's response as it lights up and charges the bait.

Currents are fluctuating all the time and there is usually a period of a few days each month when the Humboldt moves farther offshore and fingers of the Panama Current bring warmer water inshore. The sudden change can often cause fishing to ease off for a day or two, but the warmer current (called El Nino) frequently brings huge black

Deep-sea fishing, Punta Carnero

marlin and some of the largest Pacific sailfish you have ever seen. Then, after a few days, the Humboldt will move inshore again and the striped marlin return. If there is a season, it would have to be November through April, but there are striped marlin around throughout the year. Mid-April is also a good time for black marlin and the peak for this great gamefish continues through June. Sailfish aren't particularly abundant, but there's enough in the area to make life interesting.

Of course there are other species of fish including some of the largest Pacific Big-eye tuna in the world. Dolphin are plentiful at times and you can catch them until you tire of getting a bait or lure in the water.

One area is now being explored for its swordfish potential and a few of these gladiators have been boated in recent months. Inshore, you can enjoy fine sport with big jacks, roosterfish, and amberjacks. There are some rocky areas near Punta Santa Elena that are excellent for inshore fishing and there is a stretch of beach that usually turns up some good roosterfish.

Accommodations

Hotel Punta Carnero is a luxurious beach and sun resort for Ecuadorians and it just happens to be located near some of the greatest fishing grounds in the world. The hotel is built on a rocky promontory overlooking five miles of open beach in either direction and out across the Pacific.

It's a two-hour taxi ride from Guayaquil to the hotel and the last several miles are across a stretch of desert. Then, suddenly, a magnificent hotel looms up in front of you on a towering cliff. As you walk inside, the lobby is open since rain is never a problem. There's a picture window dining room that lets you gaze across the Pacific. Down below, a swimming pool rounds out the resort.

What To Take

The atmosphere at Punta Carnero is relaxed and informal. A sport shirt and slacks are perfect for dinner. The rest of the day you'll be in lightweight fishing clothes. It can get cool during some months once you round Punta Santa Elena and head offshore, so a light jacket is required. And, although it doesn't rain on shore, it can rain on the water, so bring the ever faithful rainsuit. A pair of boat shoes or sneakers will serve you well aboard the boat.

The fishing fleet is operated by Knud Holst under the banner of Pesca Tours and are used by guests of the Hotel. Knud's boats are equipped with good trolling tackle in both 50 and 80-pound-class. If you take your marlin fishing seriously, it's still a good idea to bring your own big game outfits. The striped marlin in these waters seem tougher than they do in other seas and many experienced anglers insist on 50-pound-class tackle. You can still do a job with a good quality 30 pound outfit and it's worth taking one along.

If you enjoy casting, be sure to take your own casting tackle. You can have a go at some of the offshore species (especially dolphin when they are plentiful) and also cast the shoreline. A stout spinning rod or two and plug tackle with 15-pound-test would be as good a choice as any. You can also take a flyrod if you are so inclined. If conditions are right, it's probably the best place to try for a marlin on fly.

Cost

There are a number of special fishing packages available including five days of offshore fishing with six nights at Hotel Punta Carnero for $528 per person (double occupancy). This includes transfers from the airport at Guayaquil, meals, lodging, boat, crew, bait, and tackle.

For more information contact
Adventures Unlimited

or

*Adventure Associates
150 S.E. Second Avenue
Miami, Florida 33131
Telephone: 800-327-5781
(Toll-free)*

or

*Hotel Punta Carnero
Att: Mrs. Piedad Valle
P.O. Box 5589
Guayaquil, Ecuador*

CASA MAR, COSTA RICA

Costa Rica is one of Central America's smallest, but best developed and most attractive republics. Magnificent mountain ranges run down through the center of the country, dividing the watershed between the Atlantic and the Pacific. The Eastern slope of these mountains has the deep, tropical vegetation typical of equatorial rain forests, and rain water from this region flows eastward until it is carried by the Rio Colorado and other rivers to the Caribbean Sea.

Casa Mar sits serenely on the banks of a quiet lagoon a few minutes away from the mouth of the Rio Colorado. The camp is within a mile of the Caribbean in the rugged jungle of northeastern Costa Rica, yet it is only 45 minutes from San Jose by charter aircraft.

Tarpon, Costa Rica

From mid-January through mid-May, thousands and thousands of tarpon pour through the boca or river mouth and move into the Colorado River and its associated lagoons. More fish enter through the opening at Samay just below Casa Mar. Some fish will remain in the area for a period of time, while others will move up river right away. No one knows what causes the fish to stay or move. These are the same fish, however, that enter the San Juan river and move upstream to Lake Nicaragua.

Casa Mar is managed by Bill Barnes and his wife Linda. Bill is a native Floridian who has spent years chasing tarpon in the Florida Keys as well as Central America.

He's a top-rated angler in any league and he has worked hard to build one of the finest guiding crews that you'll find anywhere in Central America. They really know how to find fish and how to catch them. And, their ability to tie knots that test 100% will surprise you.

Bill Barnes is the first one to tell you that fishing, whether at Casa Mar or elsewhere, has its ups and downs. A few weeks each season are poor by comparison to other weeks. Perhaps it's too much rain up country or some other factor that only the fish can explain, but it happens. Fortunately, the majority of the time the fishing runs from good to spectacular. Most of it is done inside the river mouth and in the various lagoons and backwaters.

In addition to tarpon, you can hang into some tremendous snook in the waters around Casa Mar. January and February are better months for snook, but they can be taken all season long in some of the deeper holes and along the shoreline.

There's one other interesting aspect of the fishing at Casa Mar that you should know about. Each year during September and October, large schools of huge snook cruise along the ocean beaches in the mild surf that is characteristic of that time of year. Last September, Gilbert Beckford took the largest snook recorded along the Atlantic Coast of Costa Rica on rod and reel. The fish weighed 44 pounds and was landed near the mouth of the Colorado River. There are also tarpon in the surf during the snook run and the weather is calm enough so that there is ample opportunity to take the boats outside the bars at the river mouth. Usually, there are thousands of tarpon milling around in this area and, if you can get out, the fishing is not to be believed.

What To Take

Life at Casa Mar is informal and completely relaxed. Lightweight fishing clothes are the main ingredient and, since you don't have to "dress" for dinner, you don't need city clothing. A good pair of boat shoes (or even two pairs) is a must and you should have a wide brimmed hat, suntan lotion or sunscreen, sunglasses, and a light windbreaker or sweater because it could get cool in the evening. You are in a rain forest, so a well-designed rainsuit should head the list of things to take.

Fishing at Casa Mar is strictly with artificial lures and casting tackle is the order of the day. Most fish are taken on spinning gear or plug casting tackle. You can use a flyrod when conditions are right, but it is best to have spinning or plug tackle for a backup.

The same gear you would use in the Florida Keys or anywhere else for tarpon would be ideal at Casa Mar. Six and one-half or seven foot plug rods will give you plenty of sport. Spinning rods should be seven to eight feet long and equipped with a large capacity spinning reel. Line tests can vary from 12-pound-test to 15-pound-test. If you're inexperienced, you might want to go to 20-pound-test.

When it comes to plugs, your selection depends on where at Casa Mar you will be fishing. In the Rio Colorado itself and near the mouth, the current is strong and the specially designed 67M Mirrolure is as good as any. You might also try Creek Chub Wiggle Divers in the larger size and the Porter Sea Hawk. Leadheaded bucktails also work. The problem is to get the lure down near the bottom in that current.

In some of the back lagoons where the flow of water isn't rapid and where the tarpon roll lazily, you can work anything from topwater darters such as Mirrolure 44M or 88M to slow sinking plugs. There are plenty of lures at Casa Mar and you can buy what you need if your own supply should dwindle.

You might also bring some light outfits along with topwater lures and some swimmers for fishing the fresh water lagoons. Here, such hard fighting species as the guapote, machaca, roncador, mojarra and other local species provide a rest from the heavier fish in the solitude of a jungle setting.

Accommodations

Casa Mar has room for about 20 guests in five double cabins with two beds in each. There is also a main lodge for dining and relaxing and each room has a private bath with hot and cold running water and showers. You can drink the specially filtered water.

The food at the camp is American style with a few native dishes thrown in on the side for the more adventurous eaters to sample. It's wholesome, delicious, and

plentiful. In fact, Bill Barnes often has several gallons of ice cream sitting in the freezer and that's something you seldom find in a remote camp.

Fishing is done from spacious 16-foot boats that are 5-feet wide. There's ample room for two anglers plus the guide in each skiff. The guides are residents of the nearby village of Colorado and know every inch of the area thoroughly.

Cost

The typical week at Casa Mar runs from Saturday to Saturday and the basic package price including round trip air fare from and to San Jose and the camp is $510 per person.

Where To Book

With a limited number of accommodations available and a relatively short season, it is best to book as early as possible. You can get more information or reserve a week by contacting:

Safari Outfitters
8 South Michigan Avenue
Chicago, Illinois 60603
Telephone: 312-346-9631

or

Casa Mar
1500 East Bay Drive
Largo, Florida 33540
Telephone: 813-584-7691

PARISMINA TARPON RANCHO, COSTA RICA

Located on the Atlantic side of Costa Rica below Casa Mar, Parismina Tarpon Rancho guards the mouth of the Parismina River. The fishing is similar to that described at Casa Mar and tackle requirements would be pretty much the same. There is also a fall snook and tarpon season in September and October.

Parismina Tarpon Rancho is operated by Jerry Tricomi, a skilled camp owner who spent over 20 years catering to fishermen in the Canadian bush before moving to Costa Rica. Jerry's home is outside of Chicago, but he has vast fishing experience in Central America.

Guests are housed in a modern, comfortable, two-story building with twin-bedded rooms, a dining room, relaxing area, and a kitchen. It's not luxurious, but it is a

comfortable fishing camp and it can handle sixteen fishermen a week.

Tarpon average between 55 and 65 pounds with only a few fish over 85 pounds and seldom any under 40 pounds. Snook run large in this part of the world and the largest taken during the special fall season was a trophy-sized 34 pounds.

Parismina operates on a Saturday to Saturday schedule and the cost, including the charter flight from and to San Jose is $500.

You can make reservations through your travel agent or the U.S. representative or write direct.

Safari Outfitters, Inc.
8 South Michigan Avenue
Chicago, Illinois 60603
Telephone: 312-346-9631

Jerry Tricomi
Parismina Tarpon Rancho
P.O. 2816
San Jose, Costa Rica.

PEZ MAYA, YUCATAN

There aren't many places in the world where you can cast a fly or light jig to tailing bonefish less than five minutes from the lodge. And, there aren't many places where you can fish 24 hours a day if that's your pleasure. Pez Maya is one of the most unique, exciting, and idyllic fishing lodges anywhere in the world. It's on a tiny, mainland island a half hour by air taxi from the airport at Cozumel across the Yucatan Channel.

Nestled in a grove of palm trees on a white sand beach, Pez Maya fits the fantasy of escape to a tropical island. More important, the lagoon behind the lodge is filled with bonefish and schools of prowling permit. The bonefish are relatively small in size, averaging perhaps three or four pounds, but there are enough fish over eight or nine pounds to make casting interesting. The tidal range is minimal in this back country and the fish are there all day long. You'll see them tailing and you'll find schools of fish weaving in and out of shoreline mangroves in search of tasty crustacea.

It's not difficult to cast a very light jig or present a small fly to these bonefish. The guides at Pez Maya are extremely knowledgeable and their eyes are like cameras with telephoto lenses. They'll spot fish for you a long way off. Normally, the guide will pole you in a Florida-designed skiff that's perfect for this type of fishing, but you also have the option of wading from time to time. We would suggest that you at least spend an hour or so each day wading for bonefish. It heightens the excitement when

Permit, Yucatan

you stalk your own fish on foot.

There are plenty of permit at Pez Maya and they will also strike a well-presented artificial jig. Getting them to take a fly isn't easy, but it has been done. If you've never tangled with a permit, you have a treat in store. Be sure to make that fact known so your guide can concentrate on getting you one.

The back flats at Pez Maya also are the home of some respectable barracuda—fish that weigh 20 pounds or more. You'll frequently see one lolling on the surface or cruising along slowly. Keep an extra rod rigged with a tube lure (made from surgical tubing) and toss the offering in front of the 'cuda. It's thrilling to watch that saber-toothed gamefish crash a hunk of tube, and the ensuing battle will be fast-paced and spectacular.

If a day on the water with only a couple of hours off for lunch and siesta hasn't exhausted you, you can wade the beachfront before dinner and cast to cruising snook, and occasional tarpon, and even permit and jacks. There's no telling what is in the surf and you can handle the assignment with either spinning or plug tackle.

Then, after dinner, you can wander down to the Boca Paila where the lagoon empties into the sea and fish some more. Huge cubera snapper as large as 40 pounds or more lurk in this narrow cut and they can often be enticed to clobber a topwater plug. Once hooked, they'll head seaward and you have a job ahead of you to chase down the beach and keep them from crossing the bar into open water. You can also hook big jacks, tarpon, snook, and other species in the boca.

What To Take

You won't need ties, jackets, or dressy clothing at Cozumel or Pez Maya. Sport shirts and slacks (or the equivalent for ladies) is ideal at Cozumel and not absolutely necessary at Pez Maya. The same lightweight fishing clothes along with a rainsuit, light jacket, and broad-brimmed hat that you would use anywhere in the tropics is ideal for Pez Maya. Don't forget sunscreen, polarized sunglasses, and insect repellent (although you will seldom need it).

It is necessary to bring your own tackle and what you use depends on your skill, preferences, and whether you want to limit your fishing to bonefish and permit or try the surf and boca as well. An ultra light spinning outfit with 4-pound-test line (possibly 6-pound-test if you're new to ultra light) is perfect for bonefish and you could probably land a permit on the same outfit if the permit were reasonably small.

It would make sense, however, to have a slightly heavier rod rigged for permit with a slightly larger bucktail. And, if you had a third rod, that should be rigged for barracuda. In the surf, you will need slightly heavier tackle. The outfit for permit or barracuda could double in brass, but an additional outfit with 12-pound-test line or possibly 15-pound-test would be the ticket. You'll need a rod with backbone to wrestle a cubera or trade blows with a tarpon or husky jack.

For bonefish, lures in the 1/8th ounce to 1/4 ounce range will be used most frequently. If you plan to fly fish, ignore the suggestions of those who recommend standard bonefish flies in a size around 1/0. Instead, take a selection of tiny patterns tied on a number 4 and number 6 hooks. All you need are basic light colors and dark colors. When the fish stop hitting the light, switch to the dark (and vice versa). The small flies really do the job better than anyting else.

Some heavier jigs for the surf and for other species are a worthwhile addition and you should have some large topwater plugs for cubera. Tube lures are the answer for barracuda.

Don't go to Pez Maya without some medium sized plugs such as 66M and 52M Mirrolures or other minnow type offerings. And, a few darters, chuggers, and poppers will add to your enjoyment.

Snook, Yucatan

Bonefish, Bahamas

Accommodations

A tour to Pez Maya includes a chance to overnight at the lovely Cabanas del Caribe Club in Cozumel, where you can relax, have dinner, and even watch the sophisticated tarpon feed on glass minnows in front of the patio. The next morning, you'll fly to Pez Maya aboard a light plane, have breakfast, and start fishing.

Three thatched-roof, Mayan style duplex cottages hide from the sun under towering palms on a white sand beach. There is also a dining room and lounge with interesting appointments and a Mayan flavor. Don't let the Mayan motif fool you. The lodge is ultra-modern and luxurious. Rooms are spacious and the baths are as modern as any at home. It's hard to believe where you are and you probably couldn't have planned it better if you did the decorating yourself.

The food is a blend of local dishes and American cuisine. It's served with a touch of elegance and it is most enjoyable.

Cost

A stay at Pez Maya includes one night and meals at Cabanas del Caribe in Cozumel, the air taxi, guides and boats, food and lodging, and transfers to and from the airport at Cozumel. Three days of fishing for two people are approximately $600. It is $800 for four days, and $1,400 for seven days (again for two people). Alcoholic beverages and gratuities are extra.

For further information contact your travel agent or

World Wide Sportsman
P.O. Box 787
Islamorada, Florida 33036
Telephone: 305-664-4615

Pez Maya
c/o Cabanas del Caribe
Cozumel, QR
Mexico

DEEP WATER CAY CLUB, BAHAMAS

The vast network of tiny islands, creeks, and shallow flats that laces the remote and beautiful East End of Grand Bahama Island provides some of the finest bonefish waters in the world. An angler could fish daily for a month and probably never pole or wade the same flat twice. The expanse of bonefish habitat is staggering and it is pure delight to explore miles of shallows without seeing another boat.

Deep Water Cay lies within two miles of Northwest Providence Channel, facing the Tongue of the Ocean. The 100-fathom-curve is that close to the pretty island that houses the Deep Water Cay Club. There are also reefs in front of the Club that harbor a variety of species. In bluewater, an angler can enjoy fine sport with marlin, blackfin and yellowfin tuna, wahoo, bonito, and other pelagic species that prowl the 100 fathom curve and the associated dropoffs.

The flats at Deep Water Cay are not limited to bonefish alone. Some areas host the elusive permit, while you can find barracuda on most of the shallow areas plus some jack crevalle and, at certain times of the year, mutton snapper.

In addition to the fabulous fishing potential, Deep Water Cay also offers excellent skindiving possibilities over the coral reefs and around the mysterious "blue holes" that lie in the nearby shallows. You can also enjoy the sandy beaches and spend time swimming, shell collecting, or beachcombing at a leisurely pace.

What To Bring

Dress at Deep Water is informal at all times. Fishing clothes are worn during the day and guests normally change for the evening. Coats and ties are not required. Don't forget a bathing suit, rain gear, a sweater or jacket, canvas shoes for wading, and hats and lotion for protection against the sun. Since you'll be traveling on small aircraft to reach the Club, it's a good idea to keep clothing needs to a minimum.

The Club maintains a small, but well-equipped tackle shop plus a full line of rental rods and equipment. It is always best, however, if you bring your own tackle. For bonefishing, you have the option of using fly tackle, spinning, or even plug casting gear. Spinning, of course, is the most popular and the ideal outfit is a light rod with 6 or possibly 8-pound-test line. If you're experienced, you may want to fish 4-pound-test. A flyrod capable of handling a weight forward 8 or 9-weight-line would normally be perfect.

It makes sense to have at least one backup outfit for bonefish and perhaps another combination or two for barracuda or permit. The trick on the flats is to have three or four rods rigged and ready all the time. Then, you're ready for what ever comes along.

If you should plan to sample the reef fishing or offshore trolling, you should bring tackle tailored to that sport. Leadheaded bucktails are the ticket for jigging the reef and the rods should handle 12 or 15-pound-test line. A 30-pound-class outfit would be the number one choice for offshore trolling. You

may want heavier tackle for blue marlin, but blues don't strike every day and you can have a lot more fun with 30-pound-class or lighter.

Accommodations

Deep Water Cay Club is a comfortable fishing lodge with many conveniences. Guests live in attractive duplex cottages complete with modern private baths. There are also two-bedroom luxury cottages with bar and kitchenette facilities available at extra cost. The main lodge boasts a comfortable lounging area with fireplace and spacious, covered porches that provide picturesque views of the surrounding sea and creeks. The dining room and bar are also located in the main lodge.

For the visiting yachtsman, there is a protected harbor with ample docking facilities. Fuel and a limited supply of fresh water are available and there are limited mechanical services. The channel into the Club is marked, but it is sometimes tricky. However, someone is usually available to lead particularly large craft through the channel.

There's also a private airstrip for visiting pilots. It's about 2,000 feet long and can handle light single or twin engine aircraft. You must, however, have permission from the Club to land. They monitor a Unicom set on 122.8 megacycles. And, amphibious planes can obtain permission to use the concrete ramp at the Club.

Cost

Guests are encouraged to arrive

and depart on a Monday or Friday. The basic bonefish package includes room, meals, boat, guide, tackle, and bait and is priced at $65 per day per person for a party of two. If you want to spend a week at the Club, the cost is $425 per person for a party of two. Charter flights are available from West Palm Beach and from Miami. The cost is about $40 per person each way. You can also charter an air taxi from Freeport to reach the Club.

For further information contact *Adventures Unlimited,*

or

Deep Water Cay Club
P.O. Box 1145
Palm Beach, Florida 33480
Telephone: 305-655-2988

WALKER'S CAY, BAHAMAS

Walker's Cay has been chronicled in the pages of angling literature almost from the time that the first sportfishing cruisers prowled the waters of the Bahamas. Through the years, the waters near Walker's have given up a respectable number of record catches, but the truly unique aspect is its location. Lying only forty-three miles northeast of Settlement Point, Grand Bahama, Walker's Cay is the northernmost island in the Bahamas. Blue water with steep dropoffs is only fifteen minutes from the dock and an offshore line of virgin coral reefs make it truly an anglers paradise. There are miles of bonefish flats and inshore reefs that rest undisturbed in the warm Bahamian sunshine.

Blue marlin, Gulf Stream

The search is on at Walker's for a blue marlin that will weigh more than 1,000 pounds. Offshore, the reef line tumbles into almost a bottomless ocean, and it is along this pronounced dropoff that billfish search for food. Blue marlin the size of a railroad car have been sighted, but none have been landed with those dimensions. In addition to the regular fare of blue marlin, these waters yield plenty of white marlin and sailfish. Wahoo are around in the spring of the year and there are king mackerel during the winter. Hundreds of species abound in this region.

Over the reefs, you are apt to find everything from amberjack, grouper, and snapper, to tuna, bonito, mackerel, and even sailfish. Deep jigging can become an addiction over these reefs.

Moving inshore, the water gets shallower and there are more reefs with smaller specimens of fish that inhabit the deeper reefs. Lighter tackle is the answer and the sport can be fast. And, there are bonefish flats. The expanse of flats isn't as large as it is in other parts of the Bahamas, but there are enough areas to pursue the bonefish. Bones in this area grow big and a ten or eleven pounder is not uncommon. Permit are scarce, but they do show occasionally. However, the flats are loaded with barracuda during the winter months and you can enjoy some of the fastest sport you've ever encountered if you toss a tube lure in any direction.

What To Take

Walker's Cay is more of a fishing resort than a fishing camp. It is luxurious in every respect and although you may spend the day in fishing clothes, you would want a sport shirt and slacks in the evening and perhaps a jacket. On the water, you can wear lightweight clothing, but you should have a rainsuit and a light jacket. During the winter months, an occasional cold front drifts across from the Florida mainland and it can get windy and cold. At these times, a warmer jacket will be most welcome.

The tackle you take depends on the fishing you intend to do. Charter boats normally carry heavy trolling tackle, but it's always good idea to bring your own. Over the reefs, you can fish bait with heavier gear or jig bucktails on spinning or plug tackle. Outfits that comfortably handle 15-pound-test line or even 20 will do the job on the deeper reefs and you can work the inside coral reefs with lines testing 10 or 12 pounds.

On the bonefish flats, 8 or 10-pound-test is fine and the same type of outfit can be used for barracuda. Be sure to bring extra line and an assortment of lures. If you expect to troll offshore, you might want to bring your own leaders and hooks.

Accommodations

The Walker's Cay Club is among the finest resorts in the Bahamas and it offers large air-conditioned rooms with private terrace as well as elegantly decorated villas if you prefer more privacy. A spacious dining room plus a large lounge and bar add to the attractions. There are two swimming pools, a television room, and a pool room. The Sea Lion Marina is a showplace with excellent docking and storage facilities plus all the conveniences of the best marina on the mainland.

There's a 2,600-foot paved airstrip equipped to handle private aircraft and aviation gas is available. A non-directional beacon operates on a frequency of 280 KHz. The club also monitors UNICOM (122.8 mgs.).

At Walker's, the cuisine is elegant and the wine list rivals any fine restaurant. Seafood delicacies and steaks head the entrees.

Cost

Walker's Cay operates on the modified American plan that includes breakfast and dinner. During the winter season, hotel rooms are approximately $36 per person, double occupancy. The daily rate for the villas are $150 double. A service charge of 15% is added to your bill.

Boat charters (including guide, tackle, and bait) are extra and depend on the size of the boat. Boston Whalers are $45 per day; 18' Starcraft are $70 per day; 22' Makos are $125 per day; and a sportfishing cruiser is $175 per day. Guides for visiting boats are $30 per day. Dockage for visiting boats is charged at the rate of $15 up to 30' and 30c for each additional foot. Other services are extra.

Contact your travel agent or
Walker's Cay Club
P.O. Box 22493
Ft. Lauderdale, Florida 33315
Telephone: 305-522-1460

LIGHT TACKLE IN BERMUDA

Rising above an underwater coral plateau some 750 miles southeast of New York, the picturesque islands of Bermuda offer fantastic light tackle fishing for a variety of species. Two hundred square miles of reefs surround the 22-mile-long main island, while Challenger Bank lies 15 miles southwest of Gibb's Hill Lighthouse and Plantagenet Bank (often known as Argus Bank) is another ten miles in the same direction. The water over these banks is about 26 fathoms deep, but the bottom drops out at the edge of Challenger and Argus to several hundred fathoms. It's the perfect setting for prowling gamefish.

The most important thing to remember about Bermuda fishing

Blackfin tuna, Bermuda

is that the season runs from May through November. During the winter and early spring months, cooler water temperatures and strong winds send many of the prime species into deeper water. Even if the weather moderates enough for you to get offshore, it's seldom very productive from December to April.

Shore Fishing

Bermuda marks the northernmost habitat of the bonefish and the gray ghost of the flats is taken regularly from July through October with the first action starting in May. Most of the fishing is in three to five feet of water over sandy bottoms and the bonefish are particularly skitterish. They average 5 to 6 pounds with an occasional 8 pounder. Bones will strike the usual small bucktails and you can also catch them on bait. Best places are Whitney Bay, Long Bay, Shelly Bay, the Causeway, and Castle Point.

Pompano trade back and forth along the South Shore beaches and Bermudans use a special chumming technique to take these scrappy crowd pleasers. The trick is to buy a few loaves of white bread (dark bread or whole wheat won't work), break it up into tiny pieces and mix it with a few cans of sardines. Wade out waist deep and toss a handful of chum seaward. Bait a small hook with a crust of bread soaked in sardine oil and wait until you see the pompano picking up the chum. Then, when there are only a couple of pieces of bread left on the water, cast the crust. The strike will be almost instantaneous.

BERMUDA CHARTER FISHING BOAT ASSOCIATION

Captain	Boat	Length	Location and Phone No.	
Herbert Adderly	Fair Lady	42'	Pembroke	Ph. 2-1191
Ronny Boys	Argosy	32'	Somerset	Ph. 8-0568
Alan Card	Sea Maid	38'	Somerset	Ph. 4-2380
Walter Darrell	Valjosha	35'	Hamilton	Ph. 2-4368
David Desilva	Tango	36'	Pembroke	Ph. 1-5876
Eugene Dublin	Maranda	45'	Hamilton	Ph. 2-5535
Boyd Gibbons	Coral Sea	37'	Somerset	Ph. 4-0506
Clyde Leseur	Challenger	45'	Paget	Ph. 1-2109
Noel Parris	Contessa	32'	Pembroke	Ph. 2-2680
Edric Pearman	Parrot	38'	St. George	Ph. 7-0620
Milton Pitman	Marlin	39'	Somerset	Ph. 4-1086
Rudy Richardson	Alrujo	42'	Flatts	Ph. 3-1275
Jimmy Saunders	Tissa R	36'	Warwick	Ph. 1-6545
Chris Smith	Ginny	33'	Southampton	Ph. 8-1466
Joe Stubbs	Troubadour	42'	Somerset	Ph. 4-0685
Clarence Welch	Hope	32'	St. George	Ph. 7-1896
George Welch	Blanche II	42'	St. George	Ph. 7-1461
Russel Young	Sea Wolfe	40'	Somerset	Ph. 4-1832

NON-MEMBERS OF THE ASSOCIATION

Buddy De Silva	Marula III		Pembroke	Ph. 2-4783
Simeon Riley	Wunderbar		Smith's	Ph. 3-0854
David Martin	Star Dust		Southampton	Ph. 2-7715
Gerald Pascoe	Capt. Bink		St. George	Ph. 7-0613
Reid Robinson	Sea Star		Hamilton	Ph. 2-5535
Rupert Swam	Cathy		Warwick	Ph. 1-6545
George Simons	Sarah J		Warwick	Ph. 2-0484

More anglers are frustrated by Bermuda's gray or mangrove snappers than all other species combined. You'll find these fussy feeders along most inshore waters and your best chances are with natural bait. However, they can be fooled with small bucktails or plugs if you have patience to try.

During the hot part of the summer, barracuda prowl the inshore flats in great numbers. You can fish for them from a small skiff or wade the flats and cast to those you see. The best lure is a homemade tube lure made by inserting a hook tied on a length of wire through 12 inches of surgical tubing. Chartreuse tubing, fluorescent red, or natural works best. Cast the tubing ahead of a 'cuda and crank it back as fast as you can. The fish should climb all over it. You can also take barracuda on a variety of plugs and bucktails.

Reef Fishing

Chumming with hog-mouthed fry and anchovies is the preferred method of fishing over the reefs. The chum is mixed with sand to help it sink and the technique is to drift a bait back in the chum slick. You also have the option of casting artificials or jigging the bottom as the boat drifts over the reef. Trolling is another favored technique.

Over the reef you can expect to catch yellowtail and gray snappers, false albacore (called mackerel in Bermuda), amberjack, horse-eye bonito (really almaco jack), and the famed Bermuda chub. If you drop a bait or bucktail to the bottom, you'll find yourself wrestling with various species of grouper.

Offshore

Bermuda's offshore waters are famous for the abundance and size of both yellowfin tuna and blackfin tuna. Almost all the IGFA records for blackfins come from this tiny Atlantic island. In addition, there are two major runs of wahoo in May and early June and again in September and October. Argus and Challenger Banks harbor some of the largest amberjack you've ever seen and there are almaco jacks, rainbow runners, dolphin, barracuda, oceanic bonito, and false albacore. Both white and blue marlin are sometimes taken, but Bermuda is not a billfish hotspot.

The more exciting method of offshore fishing is to anchor along the edge of either bank and chum with anchovies and hog-mouthed fry. Frequently, you'll see tuna

picking up pieces of chum right behind the boat and it's exciting sport to toss an anchovy with a hook in it in front of a cruising fish. You can also fish a small live bait in the chum slick for amberjack and you can cast or jig artificial lures.

Of course, much of the offshore fishing involves trolling and the boats are well-equipped with light class tackle for this sport. If you enjoy casting, it pays to have a rod or two rigged with an artificial even when you're trolling. You can often get a cast or two into a passing school of fish and a hookup is almost certain.

Blackfin tuna, Bermuda

Tackle To Take

You'll hardly ever see anyone fish Bermuda waters with tackle heavier than 30-pound-class. It's not that the fish aren't big, but rather that the local anglers emphasize light tackle and have developed the skills to handle heavyweights on featherweight gear. Most charter boats carry regulation IGFA 12 pound, 20 pound, and 30-pound-class tackle. If you want to bring your own, it's a good idea, but not absolutely necessary. However, if you want to

use fly, spinning, or plug casting tackle, you must bring your own. And, if you intend to cast, you should have your own lures.

Most inshore fishing is done with light spinning tackle and 4 or 6-pound-test lines. Light plug casting gear will also work and, if you're a fly fisherman, don't forget to include a light wand or two.

Boats To Charter

You can make your own arrangements by calling the captain or have your hotel make the arrangements for you. Members of the Bermuda Charter Fishing Boat Association charge approximately $160 for a day's fishing and will take up to six people. (See list of boats and phone number).

Tackle Rental

Fishing Tackle can be rented per day or by the week at:

BAIT AND TACKLE SHOP
Queen Street, Hamilton
Phone: 2-3828

SPORTSMAN'S SHOP
Reid Street, Hamilton
Phone: 2-6024

For further information contact:

S. L. "Pete" Perinchief
Bermuda Fishing
Information Bureau
Hamilton, Bermuda
Phone: 1-1221

You can also reach Pete Perinchief at home (Phone: 8-1257) providing he's not out fishing. Pete is Bermuda's Mr. Fishing and if you need information, he's the man who can supply it.

CLUB PACIFICO DE PANAMA

Club Pacifico de Panama sits on the inside edge of Panama's Isla de Coiba in the Gulf of Chiriqui. Coiba is an extremely large island (about the largest inshore island on the Pacific Coast from Canada to the Equator) near the Costa Rican border and about 200 miles southwest of Panama City.

The camp is in a tropical setting, rimmed by mountains in the distance and clear waters pock-marked with numerous smaller islands. Before Miami sportsman Bob Griffin conceived the idea for this camp, there was no way to realistically fish this area. Even today, you seldom if ever see another boat, other than those from camp.

Club Pacifico has been a light tackle angler's paradise. The emphasis has been placed on the lighter gear because the nearby waters abound with hundreds of species of fish from small jacks to tackle busting black marlin. It is truly a caster's haven and it can be equally rewarding for those who enjoy trolling.

More important, there are so many areas to fish that it will be years before half of them are explored. The inshore islands are home to smaller fish and an occasional big one, but when you work around those offshore islands with topwater plugs or swimmers, you won't believe what you see. Huge cubera snappers will open a hole in the water to suck in a topwater chugger, while amberjack will do the same or swallow a jig and never give it back.

During the summer months, the number of wahoo is incredible and in the spring, snappers come to the surface to feed on a small orange crab, turning the water red from the color of their bodies.

On the other hand, you can take sailfish almost anywhere, because the water (even near the islands) is deep. Then, there's Hannibal Bank, an underwater plateau with upwelling currents that keep baitfish in the area and husky predators to feed on the bait. That's one of the best spots for black marlin, striped marlin, and, of course, sailfish. At times, dolphin are everywhere and you'll get so tired of catching these great fish that you'll move off to try something else.

The key to Club Pacifico is variety. There is something to whet the appetite of every angler and enough options to keep even the most sophisticated customers coming back for more and more.

What to Take

Casual, lightweight clothing is standard at Club Pacifico. There is adequate laundry service at the Club so you can limit your fishing wardrobe. However, the Panamanian sun is strong and you should have a couple of long sleeve shirts as well as the customary short sleeve varieties. A wide-brimmed hat is a must as well as suntan lotion, lightweight raingear, sunglasses, rubber soled shoes, and that always important insect repellent.

There is some liquor available at camp, but it's always wise to cover your alcohol and tobacco needs at the dury-free shops at the gateway airports of Miami, New Orleans, or Los Angeles.

The best advice anyone can give you when you pack your tackle is to take much more than you think you will need. The Club has heavy gear for black marlin, but you must bring your own light tackle. The fish are big and strong. They will break lines as if they were kite string and they are going to eat lures. You'll land your share, but normally, the tackle takes a beating.

As a minimum, you should have two outfits for any type of fishing you might want to do. If spinning is your pleasure, you need at least a pair of outfits. At least one of them should have 15-pound-test line (or possibly 20-pound-test). Plug casters will do all right with the standard 15-pound-test plug outfits used in South Florida for tarpon and other heavyweight fish. The world of the fly fisherman is wide open and at least one flyrod should be of the heavy variety that can handle an 11 weight or 12 weight line. A 20-pound-class trolling outfit may be a welcome addition to your gear.

Beside the heavier casting tackle, you may want to take some lighter weight stuff for some of the smaller species. Tackle for putting the pressure on a largemouth bass or for handling school stripers may be ideal. Don't forget spare spools for each reel and enough bulk line to replace any that is lost or abraded.

When it comes to lures and terminal tackle, take your choice. You should have several topwater chuggers or poppers, some swimmers, and some sinking plugs and/or deep runners. Even though you are fishing light casting tackle, you may want some very large plugs for big cubera snapper or other critters that show a fondness for those offerings. You'll also need some wire leader, plenty of heavy mono leader (in two or three tests such as 50, 80, and 100), and some extra treble hooks to repair damaged plugs (if you're lucky enough to get them back at all).

Some of the more popular lures are available at the Club and can be purchased at prices comparable to list prices in the United States. And one more thing. If you want to do some deep jigging, bring a supply of white bucktails in the 2 to 4 ounce range. It's a gambler's bet that you'll go home without one of them left.

Accommodations

Club Pacifico is a modern, comfortable fishing camp with a main lodge and several spacious, duplex cottages. It is not plush, but the bedrooms are large with wall to wall carpeting, good beds, private bath, and air-conditioning.

A huge power plant generates electricity for all appliances, an ice making machine, refrigeration, and the air conditioning. All of the cottages overlook the crystalline water and a good sandy beach makes a morning or evening dip a refreshing way to begin or end a day's fishing.

The meals are typically American with steaks, chicken, beef, and seafood as the main courses. The dining area and bar are in the main lodge, and drinks may also be enjoyed on the outdoor patio.

Cost

Bookings are made on a Saturday to Saturday basis and include six full days of fishing and seven nights of lodging. The basic rate of $600 per person (double occupancy) includes all of the camp costs plus the use of a 19 foot Mako with guide. There is an additional charge of $60 for the charter flight from and to Panama City. A 32 foot Prowler and 23 foot Seacrafts are also available at a slightly increased cost.

You can obtain literature or book this trip through Safari Outfitters.

Exotics

Peacock bass, Brazil

DORADO IN PARAGUAY AND ARGENTINA

A native of South America, the dorado has earned its reputation as the toughest and most ferocious fresh-water fish. This bruising battler resembles the chinook salmon in shape and fighting qualities, but it boasts a large mouth with short, ripping teeth. Almost green in color across the back, the dorado has yellowish-orange sides and dark red fins. Weights vary, but most dorado are 15 pounds or more and some reach 60 or 65 pounds.

The wide, swift-flowing Parana River between Paraguay and

Argentina is famous for its dorado fishing and, although this species is found in other waters, the Parana gets most of the attention. Basically, dorado prefer rocks, rapids, and fast water. They seldom feed on the surface and most fish are hooked at depths ranging from 4 to 15 feet or more. Because of the rapidly moving water and the necessity of keeping a lure deep, trolling has been the favored approach to this fishing.

It should be pointed out that as more North Americans and Europeans visit the area and fish with casting tackle, the local guides are becoming increasingly convinced that casting will work. You'll need rather stout casting tackle, because you want to be able to throw a big lure and have plenty of backbone in the rod to move a husky fish against the current. The ideal gear would be the type used for casting to tarpon in Florida. Line tests between 12 and 20 pounds would be adequate.

The best dorado fishing occurs when water levels are lowest, because the fish are more concentrated and easier to find. The lowest volumes of water generally occur from July through October and if you wanted to pick the best time, it would normally be in August and September. Again, you must recognize that an unusual amount of rainfall in a given year or later rains than normal could throw the timetable off.

Local anglers show a marked preference for spoons and particularly the larger sizes such as you might use for muskies in the United States or Canada. However, one reason for the use of spoons is that they are readily available in South America and somewhat less expensive than plugs. Experts tell us that plugs are still the better choice and these should be large and seemingly indestructable. Dorado can crush many things easily with their sharp teeth and powerful jaws. Jointed plugs work better than the solid models in some places.

Fly fishing for dorado is not only possible, it has been done. You should realize, however, that it is difficult to find places to fly fish effectively and you'll be doing a lot of blind casting. If you bring a flyrod, remember that you might not get a chance to use it.

Since dorado have sharp teeth, you're going to need wire leaders. Their mouths are tough and it is often hard to get a hook in the fish or make the hook hold. For that reason, your hooks should be sharpened before use and kept sharp.

TIGER HILL SAFARI, PARAGUAY

One of the big problems for the visiting angler is the lack of accommodations near the hotspots for dorado. Tiger Hill Safaris puts together a package deal that enables you to fish the most productive rivers at the time of your visit. The tour operates the year around, but they feel that September to March is the best time on the rivers they fish.

They'll do their best to get you dorado, but you have to be flexible and willing to go on safari.

Accommodations could be in local hotels, ranch houses, or even tents. You'll need tropical weight clothing and a rainsuit for the junket and can expect warm daytime temperatures, but cooler at night.

A five day trip that includes three full days of fishing and two half days plus four nights lodging and meals is about $350 per person with two people going. The rate drops if there are three or four anglers. The safari starts at the airport in Asuncion and ends there.

If you would like to know more, contact the Braniff Outdoor Council, Braniff International, Exchange Park, Dallas, Texas or Tiger Hill Safaris, Independencia Nacional 225, Asuncion, Paraguay.

APIPE SAFARIS, ARGENTINA

One of the best haunts for big dorado is the Alto Parana near Posadas where the river is about two miles wide. This area is about 600 miles north of Buenos Aires and there are commercial flights available to the airport at Posadas. Apipe Safaris operates from April through October, but the best fishing would be in late July, August, and September.

There are no fancy hotels in this part of Argentina, but a modest and comfortable camp is located on the river. It has electricity, good furnishings, and a dining room in the main lodge. The cost of five days of fishing, six nights lodging, meals, boats, guides, and transfer from and to the airport at Posadas is $250 per person for a party of two anglers.

You can learn more about it by writing to the Braniff Outdoor Council, Braniff International, Exchange Park, Dallas, Texas or by writing directly to Apipe Safaris, Posadas, Argentina.

EL DORADO LODGE, COLOMBIA

The jungle lakes of El Dorado abound with a variety of fish including a species of pavon known as the golden bass. You may have heard of this great gamefish by another name, for the same species is called tucunare, peacock bass, and a host of other things (especially when one of them crochets your line in the brush or pops the mono with a sudden, boring surge). Expert bassmen from North America are convinced that the tucunare could drag our own largemouths and smallmouths backward through the water if the two were tied together. They are that strong.

Until recently, only a handful of "outsiders" had fished for this explosive bundle of dynamite, because there was no way to reach the areas of the Amazon these fish inhabited unless you were willing to set up your own safari. Peacock bass prefer the quiet backwaters off the main river systems and in front of El Dorado, the Vaupes River spreads deeper into the jungle, forming a series of lakes. The Vaupes is part of the famed Rio Negro system which gains momentum downstream and joins the mighty Amazon.

In addition to peacock bass, the same waters hold the huge black piranha which will reach a weight of seven pounds or more. There are also high jumping payara with a pair of fangs that fit through holes in the upper lip. You'll catch species of fish that you never suspected even existed and you'll discover that they are strong fighters ready to clobber an artificial.

Between the dry season and the rainy season, the water level can fluctuate thirty feet or more. Fishing normally begins in September and continues through April, but the best months would be in December, January, February, and the first part of March. It can be fantastic in late March or April, but this can depend on the amount of rain.

Peacock bass, Colombia

The Lodge

El Dorado Lodge is located on a landscaped clearing in the heart of an Amazonian rain forest. The lodge overlooks the lake and sits on a high knoll surrounded by fruit trees, flowers, and palms. There is a swimming pool just like any back home, and it's probably the only one in the entire Amazon.

There are several small cottages plus the main lodge. The accommodations are spacious with comfortable beds, private baths, electricity, and plenty of ice. Insects are virtually non-existent for some reason, except that there are a few chiggers if you wander off in the grassy areas. When you consider where you are, the comforts are almost unbelievable and the fishing is excellent.

For those who aren't ardent anglers or who enjoy combining fishing with sightseeing, there are a wealth of interesting things to do. You can visit neighboring Indian villages or walk in the jungle. If photography is your game, there are countless things to record on film and El Dorado has often been called a bird watcher's paradise. One aficionado sighted 40 different species in one afternoon right from the lodge. Guides are available to help you build blinds for photography or for watching animals and to cater to your wishes. You may even want to collect butterflies (the huge and brilliantly colored Amazon variety) or collect tropical fish.

What To Take

Fishing for peacock bass and the other jungle species is exciting sport and there are many options open to you from a tackle standpoint. Most visitors employ the same gear they would use for largemouths back home. This means either a bait casting outfit or a light spinning rod. Of course, it is always better to bring at least two outfits and hopefully three or four. You'll have extra gear in case something breaks, but you can also be rigged with two or three different lures at the same time and only have to change rods to try a different offering.

The terrain is rugged and the bass are tough. They are going to break lines and you can expect them to dive for the nearest cover when hooked. That means you should have spare spools with extra line and perhaps a bulk spool or two just in case.

Most of the fishing is casting the shoreline or tossing a lure in the midst of a school of feeding bass. However, there are times when some anglers troll and you may want to do this as well. Fly fishermen can have a great time and regular bass bugging tackle is the ticket. Take both a floating and a sinking line and you're in business. Flies should be topwater poppers and large, saltwater type streamers. These fish will hit streamers and bucktails from a couple inches to six inches or more.

When it comes to lures, you have a wide choice. The greatest sport is to take these fish on topwater baits. Poppers, chuggers, topwater swimmers, and darters all work well. You should also take a variety of deeper running plugs and a selection of spoons such as the famed Dardevle.

The peacock bass doesn't have any teeth, but many other species do. Most anglers take wire leader or plastic coated wire leader material. You'll save some lures by using this protection, but you'll hook fewer fish and experience fewer strikes. A short length of heavier monofilament is a fair compromise. It will cost you some lures, but you'll have a lot more action.

The weather is warm and the sun is strong. You'll require a broad-brimmed hat, sun screen lotion, and even long-sleeved shirts for protection from the sun. A light jacket is always advisable and a rainsuit is a must. Other than that, comfortable, informal clothes are the order of the day.

How To Get There

Reaching El Dorado is relatively easy. You fly on a jet from Miami to Bogota, overnight, and then by charter aircraft to the little village of Miraflores near the border of Venezuela and Brazil. You'll be met at Miraflores and taken by boat to the lodge. The boat trip is about two hours and it will be an exciting introduction into the Amazon jungle.

Cost

The cost of an eight-day, seven-night trip to El Dorado is a little over $500, including air transportation from Bogota to the lodge and return, hotels in Bogota, and all transfers.

For further information contact

your travel agent or Adventures Associates. Or you may write direct to

El Dorado Lodge
Att: Willis Crawley
Miraflores
Vaupes, Colombia
South America

transcends international borders. Equally important, your hosts in the land that you are visiting are more than anxious to show you the beauty of their country and have you share in nature's wonders.

Whether your trip is to Western or Eastern Europe, there are plenty of angling waters available to you. Little needs to be said about the

is a much better idea to take your own. An eight-foot flyrod that breaks down into several sections takes very little room in a suitcase and a flyreel with a floating line can almost be carried in your coat pocket. All you need are some leaders (nine foot 3X, 4X, and 5X are a good starting point) and a couple of boxes of flies. Take an assortment of streamers, bucktails, wets, and nymphs, as well as a few dry flies.

Most countries require you to have two types of licenses and they are not only reasonably priced, but require little formality to obtain. One license is from the country and the other grants you the right to fish specific waters. The water rights are often controlled by the hotel at which you might stay or by a local angling association.

In Addition

Salmon fishing, Driva River, Norway

EUROPE ON BUSINESS? PACK A ROD!

By asking only one or two questions, you could very well enrich any business trip to Europe and add new dimensions to your angling experiences. Most European countries offer quality trout fishing within relatively easy access of major cities and it's often a matter of making your interests known. Fishermen speak a common language and share a mutual understanding that

spectacular fishing in Scandinavia or the traditional approach to the sport in the British Isles. Yet, nations such as Spain, France, Italy, Austria, Yugoslavia, and Germany harbor delightful streams where you can counter jet lag and refresh the spirit while floating a fly for brown trout or transplanted rainbows. Keep in mind that our own brown trout are really native to Central Europe.

Equipment is normally available wherever you choose to fish, but it

You will discover that your business contacts in the country you visit will normally be pleased to assist you in making fishing arrangements and many of these men can guide you to the best waters. It's not a bad idea to ask your host to join you. No matter where you travel, it doesn't take long to ferret out the local angling expert. His reputation has been founded on results and he will normally be delighted to help you.

You may enjoy doing a little research on European fishing before your forthcoming trip. To assist you, we have listed sources of information both here and in the country you plan to visit. A day or two on a remote European stream or on a river that flows through an historic town can be the highlight of your business trip and an unparalleled way to relax from the pressures of daily activity.

COUNTRY	IN THE UNITED STATES	ABROAD
Austria	Austrian National Tourist Office, 545 5th Ave., N.Y., N.Y., 10017 212-697-0651	Osterreichische Fischereigesellschaft A-1010 Wien 1, Elisabethstrasse 22. Tel. 222 56 52 48. Verband des Osterreichischen Arbeiter-Fischerei-Vereine, A-1080 Wien VIII, Lenaugasse 14. Tel. 222 43 21 76.
Belgium	Belgian National Tourist Office, 750 5th Ave., N.Y., N.Y., 582-1750	Confederation des Pecheurs a la Linge, Place Jean Jacob, 1, 1000 Brussels, Belgium. / or the Regional Office of Tourism.
Bulgaria	Bulgarian Tourist Office, 50 E. 42 St., N.Y., N.Y. 10017 661-5733	Balkantourist, 1 Lenin Square, Sofia, Bulgaria. Att: Overseas Dept.
Czechoslovakia	Czechoslovak Travel Bureau—"Cedok", 10 E. 40 St., N.Y., N.Y. 10017 689-9720	Cedok, Dept. of Fishing, Panska 5, 11135, Prague, Czech.
Denmark	Danish National Tourist Office, 505 5th Ave., N.Y., N.Y., 687-5605	Fiskeriinspektoren, Borgergade 16, 1300 Copenhagen K. Tel. 01 11 05 19. / or Denmark's Sports Fishing Assoc— Danmark Sportsfiskerforbunds Sekretariat, Sydkajen, P.O. Box 194, Vejle, Denmark.
England	British Tourist Authority, 680 5th Ave., N.Y., N.Y. 581-4700.	BTA, 64 St. James' Street, London SW1A INF. Tel. 01-629-9191.
Finland	Finnish National Tourist Office, 505 5th Ave., N.Y., N.Y. 687-5605	Finnish Tourist Board, Kluuvikatu 10, Helsinki 10. Tel. 650155 / or the Real Estate Office of the National Board of Forestry, Uudenmaankatu 4-6, F, SF-00120, Helsinki 12. Tel. 601511.
France	French Government Tourist Office, 610 5th Ave., N.Y., N.Y. 757-1125	Tourist Information / or the Town Hall ("Mairie").
Germany	German National Tourist Office, 630 5th Ave., N.Y., N.Y. 757-8570	Verband Deutscher Sportfischer, D 605, Offenbach, Waldstrasse 6.
Iceland	Icelandic Airlines, Tourist Information, 610 5th Ave., N.Y., N.Y. 757-8585	Icelandic Airlines, Vesturgata 2, Rekjavik 20200.
Ireland	Irish Tourist Board, 590 5th Ave., N.Y., N.Y. 246-7400	Irish Tourist Board, Angling Information Service, Baggot Street Bridge, Dublin 2. Tel. 65871.

COUNTRY	IN THE UNITED STATES	ABROAD
Italy	Italian Advisory Tourist Office, Scandanavia House, 505 5th Ave., N.Y., N.Y. 687-5605	Federazione Italiana della Pesca Sportiva, Viale Tiziano 70, Rome, Italy. Tel. 39-4754/35-5684.
Netherlands	Netherlands National Tourist Office, 505 5th Ave., N.Y., N.Y. 245-5320	General Angler's Association, Weyeringschaus 106, Amsterdam. Tel. 020-62874.
Norway	Norwegian National Tourist Office, 505 5th Ave., N.Y., N.Y. 687-5605	Norway Travel Association, H Heyerdahlsgathe 1 Oslo, 1 Norway. Tel 42-70-44.
Poland	"Orbis," Polish Travel Office, Information Bureau, 500 5th Ave., N.Y., N.Y. 524-4152	"Orbis," Polish Travel Office, Warszawa, u1, Bracka 16. Tel. 26 02 71.
Romania	"Carpati," Romanian National Tourist Office, 500 5th Ave, Room 328, N.Y., N.Y. 10035 524-6951	"Carpati," National Tourist Office, Bucharest, Hunting Dept., 7, Maghern. Tel. 14-51-60.
Scotland	British Tourist Board (see England).	Scottish Tourist Board, 2 Rutland Place, Edinburgh EH12YU. Tel. 031-332-2433.
Spain	Spanish National Tourist Office, 589 5th Ave., N.Y., N.Y. 759-3842	Administracion Turistica Espanola, Arda. del Generalisimo, 39, Madrid. Tel. 2796000.
Sweden	Swedish Travel Information, 505 5th Ave., N.Y., N.Y. 687-5605	Swedish Tourist Traffic Assoc., Box 7306 S-10385, Stockholm 7. Tel. 08-22 32 80.
Switzerland	Swiss National Tourist Office, 10 W. 49 St., N.Y., N.Y. 10017 757-5944	Office national suisse de tourisme, Zurich, Bahnhofplatz 9. Tel. 01-23-57-13.
Wales	British Tourist Authority (see England).	Wales Tourist Board, High Street, Llandaff, Cardiff. Tel. 566133.
Yugoslavia	Yugoslav National Tourist Office, 509 Madison Avenue, N.Y., N.Y. 10022 753-8710	Turisticki Savez Jugoslavije, Beograd Mose Pijade 8/IV, P. FAH 595, Jugoslavie.

THE NATIONAL FISH STAMP PROGRAM

Noting that "The Greatest Sporting Goods Store In The World" must lead in the preservation of the wilderness and its critical impact on the reproduction cycle, Harold G. Haskell, Jr., President of Abercrombie & Fitch conceived the idea of a National Fish Stamp Program. Similar to the Federal Duck Stamp program that is familiar to anyone who has ever pointed a shotgun at a flight of ducks or tried to isolate a quail from an exploding covey, the Fish Stamp will give fishermen of America an opportunity to actively contribute to the conservation and beneficial control of our endangered sporting fish and their environs.

preservation and conservation of America's game and fish populations. In 1974, Trout Unlimited, the National Recreation and Park Association, and the International Atlantic Salmon Foundation were the recipients of the donation. Equally deserving organizations and agencies will be selected in future years.

The Fish Stamp is sold to collectors in kit form that includes a numbered and signed reproduction of the original artwork, 100 special First Day Cover envelopes, and 100 finely engraved stamps. To insure the ever increasing value of the prints over the years, each issue is limited to 500.

Wildlife artist Don Crowley, whose work was selected from among many other submissions, was commissioned to render the original painting for the first Stamp. Each year, Abercrombie & Fitch will conduct a national contest to select the painting to be honored on the stamp.

If you recognize the responsibility of doing something now to help insure quality fishing for the generations that follow, the National Fish Stamp Program is deserving of your attention.

To order, send your name and address and check or money order for $100, made out to Abercrombie & Fitch - Fish Stamp, to P.O. Box 4266, Grand Central Station, New York, N.Y. 10017. You may charge your Fish Stamp kit to your A&F Charge Account, or to your American Express, Bank Americard, Diners Club, Master Charge, and you may telephone in your order.

Fish Stamp painted by Don Crowley

To make his dream a reality, Hal Haskell announced that A&F would donate twenty-five percent of the revenues from the stamp program to non-profit organizations dedicated to the

PLAN YOUR TRIP CAREFULLY

No one can predict the vagaries of nature or the daily movements of fish with unerring accuracy, but advanced planning coupled with full disclosure of your requirements can often turn the odds in your favor. It's as simple as letting your gillie, guide, charter captain or the lodge owner know the species you particularly want to catch and the angling methods you intend to use. At the same time, tell your host whether you are an experienced angler or a novice.

This information is frequently vital to a successful trip. For one thing, the lodge owner or guide can tell you the best time of year for the species you seek and the method you intend to use. If, for example, you wanted to dry fly fish for trophy brown trout in Chile on the Cumilahue River, your timing would be off unless you arrived from mid-January through mid-February. On the other hand, if you wanted big rainbow trout in that same river, you should be casting a streamer fly in November and early December.

There are countless examples, but it tapers down to one salient fact: the man on the scene knows his waters. Let him tell you when to come if you are looking for a specialized type of fishing.

It's no secret that some guides are much more patient and more tolerant of beginners, enjoying the challenge of helping these newcomers catch fish. Other skippers prefer only veteran anglers. By disclosing your personal degree of competency, you will frequently be assigned a guide who is best qualified to fill your needs.

This is particularly true for the light tackle enthusiast who might want to tackle a sailfish on plug casting tackle or a tarpon on a flyrod. At any lodge, certain guides will be more experienced in the use of different types of tackle and the lodge owner is only too willing to assign them to you, if he knows what you plan to do.

The greatest advertisement for any fishing resort is a satisfied angler. Everyone is on your side and wants to make you the angler of the year, but they need this vital information to help them. So, when you inquire about a fishing possibility or book a trip, take the time to make your plans known. That way you have the whole team working for you.

IMPROVING YOUR TECHNIQUE

Old Ike Walton once turned to the legions of fishermen of his day who sallied forth on stream or brook to fool the wily trout or tease the mighty salmon into taking a fly and calmly announced that no man is born an angler. He may just as well have added that no man (or woman for that matter) is born a fly fisherman.

Learning to cast a fly is easy, but it requires two things: a properly matched outfit and someone to keep you from falling victim to bad casting habits before they become ingrained. Since most of us are forever struggling to keep our backcasts airborne while we push harder on the forward cast to steal more distance, some qualified instruction would probably be a welcome respite.

Knot-tying at the Orvis Fly Fishing School

Recognizing that no one ever fully masters the flyrod and that most of us would love to improve the delicacy of our presentation or add those feet of distance, leading tackle companies began to design courses for the fly fisherman. At first, the emphasis was primarily on casting, and casting is still a vital part of the instruction. However, some of the schools have gone beyond the casting phase and teach streamcraft, knots, and basically, how to fish. They pack a great deal of information into a few days and the instructors are well-qualified to help with almost any angling problem.

Courses are scattered throughout the country and run for various lengths of time ranging from a two-day course to a full week or more. Costs also vary, but you can figure on a $100 minimum up to about $400. Of course, there are often extras such as travel arrangements, and some courses do not include food or accommodations. The fishing schools are tailored to teach the beginner or help the veteran improve certain phases of his technique. Many also delight in helping women learn to flycast. In fact, most instructors readily admit that the ladies are better pupils because they want to learn and they don't let their egos stand in the way.

Even if they don't participate, wives and youngsters are generally welcome at the fishing schools and there are often interesting activities available to keep them occupied while you learn to cast.

If you would like more information on the locations of the various schools, dates, and the cost, we suggest you write directly to any or all of the following:

*BERKLEY FLY FISHING
HOLIDAYS
Berkley and Company
Spirit Lake, Iowa 51360*

*FENWICK INSTITUTE
OF FLY FISHING
P.O. Box 729
Westminster, California 92683*

*GARCIA FLY FISHING
SCHOOLS
c/o The American Sportsman's
Club, Inc.
650 South Lipan Street
Denver, Colorado 80223*

*ORVIS FLY FISHING SCHOOL
Orvis Company
Manchester, Vermont 05254*

Casting practice, Orvis Fly Fishing School

PREPARING AND PACKING YOUR FISHING TACKLE

Some of the finest waters and many of the most rewarding fishing opportunities are located hundreds of miles from the nearest tackle shop. Replacement tackle is generally out of the question, so it is imperative that you carry enough gear to adequately handle the assignment and pack your equipment so that it arrives at your destination intact.

Any experienced angler will quickly confirm that lodge owners find it difficult to maintain a supply of tackle for sale or rent. Even if the lodge does have a few rods and reels for emergency use, this equipment has usually seen better days and may take away from your total enjoyment.

The best approach is to pack more tackle than you think you will need. Then you're covered for any eventuality, and if there is a local lure or two that is particularly effective, you can buy it on the scene.

Our own travels in pursuit of fishing encompass more than 100,000 miles each year and we would like to suggest some general guidelines based on this experience which you may find helpful.

1. Most fishing tackle in the United States is relatively inexpensive, especially when compared to the costs for the same equipment elsewhere in the world. For that reason, it makes sense to buy your tackle at home before you depart on a trip. You will also find a greater selection of gear at your favorite tackle shop. When you consider the cost of traveling to a remote region for spectacular fishing, a modest investment in adequate tackle is the best insurance you have for a succesful trip.

2. New fishing tackle is always a delight to use, but you should take the time to test each item at home first. You'll have a chance to learn how to handle it before you leave on your trip and, should the tackle malfunction, you can have it repaired or replaced before you depart. It's the same principle as breaking in a pair of walking shoes before taking a major hike.

3. Even if you don't use it, we believe you can never have too much tackle with you. If something is going to break or fail, it will invariably happen when you're a long way from a tackle shop. Basically, you should carry at least two outfits for each type of fishing you expect to do. A backup outfit can save the day if something happens to your favorite rod and reel.

4. Before you begin to pack your tackle, each item should be inspected carefully, Reels must be cleaned and lubricated. At the same time, check the drag on each reel to make certain it is smooth. If you use spinning tackle, clean and lubricate the bail roller and its bushing so that it will roll under pressure and prevent damage to your line. Take a close look at each rod, checking to see that the guides are not nicked or grooved and that the wraps are not coming loose. Take an old nylon stocking and pull it through each guide. If the nylon snags, the guide will fray or cut a line and should be replaced.

5. New line is the cheapest and best insurance you can buy for landing a trophy fish, yet most anglers seem content to use monofilament that is already a few years old. Equally important, these same fishermen frequently embark on a vacation with reels that are only half-filled with line. To an experienced fisherman, line is a vital commodity. Before each trip, knowledgeable anglers refill each reel and extra spool. In addition, they pack bulk line in the breaking strengths they normally use. If you use Dacron line on your conventional reels, it still makes sense to carry an extra spool of line. And, fly fishermen should always take an extra flyline or two, just in case the line in use becomes damaged or even lost on a big fish.

6. The fish in remote regions are often big and unsophisticated. They frequently show little mercy on an offering and it is easy for an angler to wade through a seemingly adequate supply of flies or lures in a very short period of time. Particularly where light tackle comes into play, you must consider lures expendable. In choosing the right lures, you need both variety and depth. The best method of making a selection is to pack two to three times as many artificials as you think you'll need of the recommended patterns and styles. Then, just to be sure, throw in a variety of other lures that may work. And remember, if you're using plugs, to cover various levels of water from deep to shallow to the surface. The same theory applies to fly patterns.

7. Big fish frequently damage lures, but if you have spare hooks, split rings, and other parts, you can repair the artificials on the spot and use them if you run out of a particular model. At the same time, you should carry spare parts for your reels and a repair kit that includes various tools such as screwdrivers, pliers, vise grips, hemostats, a few extra guides for your rods, and enough cements and adhesives to patch anything. You'll also discover that some waterproof felt tip markers in a few basic colors will work wonders on transforming a lure into a preferred color or shading combination.

8. If you will need waders or hipboots on your trip, test them beforehand to insure that they do not leak. When you pack your waders, be sure to include a repair kit. Keep in mind that Space Age adhesives such as Miracle Patch can be applied with the heat of a match or candle and it will make a marvelous repair. There's nothing more uncomfortable than leaking boots or waders, so if you own an extra pair, take them along. Even if you have to pay a few dollars overweight on an airline, it can be a valuable investment if you should happen to tear your first pair beyond the point of repair.

9. Everyone has their own method of assembling tackle for packing. An effective way is to set up a bridge table or select another area where you can lay out each item before packing. After all the tackle is on display, look at it closely. At the same time, try to anticipate your needs again and study your checkoff list. Make certain that there is a reel or two for every rod and that you haven't forgotten incidental items such as leader material or insect repellent. When you're certain that you have

everything you will need, you're ready to do the actual packing.

10. How you pack your tackle depends on your method of travel, the equipment you must take, and your own personal preferences. The cardinal rule, however, is that all tackle must be packed carefully so it arrives at your destination in perfect condition. In many cases, you will be flying to your fishing paradise aboard both commercial airliners and charter flights. There are some travelers who claim that if you can pack your tackle to survive baggage handlers, it will endure anything.

11. We recommend that your fishing rods be packed in a sturdy container specially designed for fishing rods and made from high impact plastic or metal. These are available at the better tackle shops or you can make your own from a length of PVC plastic pipe and two end caps. A handle can be bolted into the plastic pipe for ease of carrying. It is important that any rod case have a lock on it so that it cannot be opened inadvertently.

12. The secret of packing rods so they won't break is a roll of masking tape. Lay your rods on the floor and align each rod so that the butt of at least one rod extends beyond the tips of the others on each side. Then tape the rods together so that they cannot shift. If a rod tip extends beyond the butt on either side, you can bet that it will arrive broken. Rainsuits, fly vests (with the fly boxes removed from the pockets) or similar items can be wrapped around the rods to help protect them and to take up any slack in the container.

13. Reels should be packed in your suitcase with care, so that there is padding on every side. Underwear, wool socks, or other clothing items make excellent padding. If you are taking spinning reels, be sure to unscrew the handles to prevent them from being broken or bent and, if the bail folds down into a traveling position, make sure this is done before packing.

14. Some anglers prefer to carry a tackle box for lures and accessories, while others are quite content with unbreakable plastic boxes that can be carried in a canvas bag. We prefer the second method and have found through trial and error that Vlchek Tuff Tainers made from crushproof polypropylene are among the strongest containers on the market today. These plastic boxes come in a variety of sizes and configurations and can be used for lures and accessories. If you prefer a tackle box, make sure you can lock it from the outside. Lately, a few tackle boxes seem to disappear in transit. If you plan to carry a tackle box, lock it and then pack it again in a plain cardboard container or a soft canvas bag. If a baggage handler cannot recognize it as a tackle box, it has a better chance of getting through.

15. Your name and home address should be plainly lettered on your rod case, tackle box, soft canvas bags, and any other baggage you use to transport tackle.

PRESERVING YOUR TROPHY

There's no better way to remember a particular fishing trip than to have a trophy mounted and hung on the wall of your den or office. It's sometimes hard to realize this in a remote area where you are living the adventure, but once you get back home, you often wish you had brought a fish back with you.

Although they only process marine specimens, we asked Pflueger Marine Taxidermy to tell us how a sportsman can get his trophy to the taxidermist from any corner of the world. Pflueger has now processed over one million fish representing 610 species from every fishing hole in the world.

Most fishing lodges represent Pflueger or another taxidermist and can make arrangements to have your fish mounted. If you are going to an area where there may not be a representative, the best policy is to check with Pflueger in advance and they will tell you specifically how to get the fish back. In spite of their size and the number of fish they process, they are delighted to help individual anglers.

Supposing, however, that you hadn't planned to have a fish mounted, but you managed to land a trophy and decided on the spot to preserve it. Your first task is to keep the fish in the best condition possible and as undamaged as you can. Minimize gaff holes, damage to the fins, or any other part of the fish. If possible, the fish should be iced or at least kept cool and moist. It should remain that way until you

can get it to a place with freezer facilities. Once the fish is frozen solid, most of your concern is over. It can be packed in any insulating material (including newspapers) and shipped by air to Pflueger in Miami or any other taxidermist. Or you can have the fish sent to your hometown in the frozen condition and then to the taxidermist. Pflueger, for example, receives fish by air from all over the world on a daily basis. The package should be marked with their address and telephone number, and there should be instructions on the outside of the package to phone Pflueger upon arrival. In spite of the fact that the Miami airport is extremely busy, cargo personnel have a warm spot in their hearts for fishermen and usually call Pflueger right away. A truck is immediately dispatched to pick up the package. Your name should be on the inside and the outside of the package along with your address and telephone number.

There are places in the world where it is impossible to keep a fish cool or freeze it. When you encounter those situations, the solution is to have the fish skinned. It's not really complicated. Use a sharp knife and make an incision along the lateral line of the fish from head to tail *on one side only.* Lift the skin up with your fingers and work the knife along the underside of the skin, separating it from the flesh. When you have done the top portion, do the same thing to the bottom half. Remember that tail, fins, and head must remain with the skin. Once you have finished one side, turn the fish over and do the other. When the skin has been removed, use the rounded portion of the

knife point to scrape as much flesh from the skin as possible.

After the flesh has been removed (and the taxidermist doesn't really expect an expert job), the inside of the skin should be salted. It's important to rub the salt into every area of the flesh part of the skin. Put the skin outdoors with the flesh side out and let it dry for 24 hours in the sun. Now pick up the skin and shake it vigorously so that all the loose salt will fall free. Re-salt the skin by hand, rubbing the salt into every part. Roll the skin up loosely and store it in a plastic bag until it can be shipped.

The mailing address for Pflueger Marine Taxidermy is P.O. Box 310, Hallandale, Florida 33009. The telephone number (and the one that should be on the outside of the package) is 305-945-4101. Someone is on duty from 8:00 A.M. until 9:00 P.M. 365 days a year. During the night, there is a reliable answering service where any message can be stored until morning.

IT CAN HAPPEN TO ANYONE

Whether you prefer to call it mal de mer, seasickness, or, more correctly, motion sickness, nothing can ruin a day on the water faster than that sudden feeling of queasiness. Yawning, lethargy, and nausea are often forerunners of the more serious symptoms that follow.

Basically, motion sickness results from over stimulation and an unusually sensitive reaction of the semi-circular canals in our inner ear. These canals, found in the labyrinth of the ear, help us to keep our balance under normal circumstances, but in some people, they respond adversely to unfamiliar motion.

Today, there are a host of drugs on the market that help to prevent motion sickness and most can be purchased without a prescription. If there is any doubt that you might be affected by motion sickness, don't hesitate to take the pills. Your family physician can recommend the best type of pills for your needs. Some medications will make you drowsy, but there are a number of new remedies on the market such as Triptone that don't seem to produce any noticeable side effects.

There are often contributing factors to seasickness besides the motion of the boat. Usually, you've had little sleep the night before and there is an undercurrent of excitement caused by the anticipation of a great day on the water. Frequently, an angler will bolt a big breakfast that may include foods that he normally doesn't eat. There will be plenty of food on the boat because everyone knows that a day on the water helps to build an appetite.

Experts advise that the best way to help prevent seasickness is to limit the amount of alcoholic intake the night before and get plenty of rest. Start the day with a light breakfast and watch your diet during the course of the time you're on the water. There's plenty of time to celebrate when you get back to port.

If you begin to suspect that you are getting sick, don't go below decks to lie down. Instead, get topside as

fast as practical and stay up in the fresh air. If the boat has a bridge, get up there. Don't do any work or play games such as cards that require eye concentration. Instead, let your eyes wander to the horizon and try to keep from focusing on any specific object. You'll also find that soda crackers sometimes have a settling effect on your stomach.

If you do get sick, watch your diet closely and limit it to liquids and perhaps some soda crackers. Surprisingly, you'll find that the minute the boat reaches the inlet and enters the sheltered waters of the estuary, your illness may miraculously disappear.

Tarpon at Casa Mar

AN OUNCE OF PREVENTION

If you pursue outdoor activities in the North Country, you are going to encounter the black fly. No one can successfully predict when they will emerge, how long they'll be around, or how abundant they'll be, because all of these details depend on the weather. Therefore, it's always best to plan on squadrons of black flies being in the area you plan to visit and take adequate precautions to minimize the discomfort.

Black flies totally ignore some people, but there are other outdoorsmen who might even get an allergic reaction from a single black fly bite. Unlike mosquitos, black flies seldom go indoors and they are usually encountered in the woods or along brushy terrain. If you're on the water a short distance from shore, you're usually out of the discomfort zone, and should you decide to have shorelunch, pick an area exposed to the prevailing breeze. Windy points are best.

When you're in black fly country, an ounce of prevention is the best medicine. Start by eliminating the use of shaving lotions, hair sprays, colognes, or other toiletry items that have a distinct aroma. These attract black flies. You'll find that bright or light colored clothing tends to repel black flies, while the darker colors attract these insects.

Although black flies can bite right through your clothing (assuming you are wearing lightweight clothes), the main menace comes when they find an exposed area. For that reason, it's best to secure pants legs, cuffs, and collars. You can do this easily with a roll of masking tape or a few large rubber bands. A handkerchief doused in insect repellent and tied around the neck is also a valuable ally.

You're going to need an adequate supply of insect repellent and it is best to carry both the aerosol spray and the lotion. The spray can be used on your clothes, while the lotion is ideal for exposed skin areas.

Another trick or two worth remembering is to carry a pair of cotton gloves to protect your hands. These can be sprayed with repellent and will help. Some fine mesh netting that can be placed over your hat and head will keep the pesky critters away from your face and neck.

Most of us who enjoy the fabulous North Country fishing or hunting, accept the black fly as part of the cost and assume that sooner or later, some of those pests are going to bite us. For that reason, we will usually carry some anti-histamine capsules prescribed by our physician to help relieve the itching and some topical ointment such as hydrocortisone. It helps to be prepared.

These anti-inflammatory medications alleviate itching and can be used for insect bites in almost any corner of the world. They should be part of your permanent medical or travel kit. If, by chance, you are caught without any medication and the bites are really killing you, try this trick. With a piece of cloth, apply water as hot as you can stand to the bite. The idea is to superheat the bite for three or four minutes. After that it shouldn't bother you for up to four hours.

NOTATIONS

The Giant Sable Antelope of Angola

Marvin Davis

A pen-and-ink drawing by Marvin Davis. *To obtain a signed and numbered print suitable for framing, see p. 188.*

HUNTING

Upland Shooting
Tallawahee Plantation, Georgia
Grouse Shooting in Scotland
Driven Partridge Shooting in Spain

Water Fowl
James Bay, Canada
Club de Patos, Yucatan
Colombian Dove and Duck Hunting

Big Game
The Full African Safari
The African Short Hunt
Mixed Bag in Alaska
Mountain Hunting in Iran
Elk and Mule Deer in Wyoming
Tahr and Chamois in New Zealand

On Firearms
Preparing For Your Hunt
Traveling With Firearms

Upland Shooting

TALLAWAHEE PLANTATION, GEORGIA

There's nothing more exhilarating to a wing shooter than the explosive eruption of a covey of quail in front of a pair of working dogs. Add a crisp morning to the setting, 5,000 acres of superb habitat and the scene is set at Tallawahee Plantation outside of Dawson, Georgia.

Both wild and carefully conditioned raised birds offer the perfect challenge at Tallawahee, where carefully managed hunting areas intersperse thousands of acres of croplands and native forests. Farming operations on this beautiful plantation have always been tailored to complement and expand the traditionally large population of game birds.

A day at Tallawahee begins with a hearty breakfast as the excitement for the day starts to fill the air. Your guide and four to six bird dogs are waiting in a special vehicle designed for hunting comfort to take you to some of the most inspiring acreage you've ever walked across. As the dogs start to work, anticipation gives way to the beauty of the scene and you are ready for the first covey of quail.

The season at Tallawahee is particularly long, starting in October and running through March. Two or three days of hunting can be an enjoyable break from your normal work routine.

Quail shooting, Georgia

Accommodations

The lodge and adjacent sleeping quarters are constructed of wide, rough cut and hand-planed pecky cypress. Many of the hand-hewn timbers come from century-old tenant houses and make a unique blend adding to the rustic atmosphere. Services are excellent and the lady in your life will be very much at home here.

Dinner is bountiful and features a variety of dishes prepared in the Southern tradition. After the sumptuous meal, there's time left to sit around the fireplace, enjoy the recreation and game rooms, or drop in at the pro shop and chat.

What To Take

Comfortable field clothing is the prescription for hunting. A pair of well-broken in boots are a must. Your regular hunting trousers or a pair of faced hunting pants are ideal. Since the season runs from October to March, the weather is going to vary considerably. You should be prepared for chilly mornings and possibly a cold day.

In the evening, dress is still informal and would be similar to that worn at any hunting club.

Preserve licenses and all-gauge shotgun shells are available, but you should bring your own shotgun and shells.

Cost

One full day's hunting with the privilege of bagging 12 quail, guide service, vehicle, dogs, food, and lodging are approximately $125. A non-shooting guest accompanying you would be billed at $40 per day. Extra birds bagged are $3.75

each. Commercial air transportation is available into Albany, Georgia and there is a charge of $25 per car for transfer to and from the plantation. Private aircraft may fly into the field at Dawson and the pickup charge is $5.00.

For further information: Adventures Unlimited.

GROUSE SHOOTING IN SCOTLAND

Grouse shooting on the moors of Scotland is legendary, a once-in-a-lifetime experience. The sport takes place in mountainous country and while very little walking is required, it often can be strenuous. Grouse are completely wild birds and can neither be reared in captivity nor fed artificially. Heather is the primary diet the year round.

The prime hunting season is from mid-August through the beginning of October. After that, it is difficult to drive the birds. During September, it is easier to get the birds airborne, but they are easier to hit in August. Hunts are organized to take these factors into consideration. More beaters are used in August, but longer drives are the answer as the season progresses.

Each hunt is under the personal direction of Major Neil Ramsay of the Scots Guards and are held on his 11,000 acre country home called Farleyer near Aberfeldy in Perthshire. There are five separate beats on this property. A beat, by the way, is the hunting area for one day. In addition, the Major also arranges for hunts on adjacent

property. You can expect four to seven drives in a day depending on the ground and the length of the drives.

The number of birds that can be expected depends on several factors, not the least of which is weather conditions. The Major tells us that an excellent team of guns on a perfect day might take 100 brace on certain beats. A poor team in a gale force wind following a poor hatch would probably take less than 25 brace. Forty brace is a respectable average.

The latest long term survey of grouse habits and requirements shows that nearly every moor in Scotland has too little hunting pressure to ever reach its optimum. Those properties that are shot over continuously produce a much better average. If grouse are not harvested, the surplus birds will be pushed out of their breeding area and will subsequently perish.

Unlike other types of driven hunts, those for grouse remain excellent throughout the season, because the birds are difficult to bring down and equally difficult to drive. Most hunters estimate a take of five to eight percent of the birds seen. Only seven hunts a season are arranged at Farleyer.

Accommodations

Each party consists of a team of eight guns. Lodging is at Farleyer, which is a comfortable country house on pleasant grounds. There are seven double rooms and seven bathrooms set aside for the hunting parties plus two single rooms. For those who hunt neighboring properties, accommodations are available at the Huntingtower

Hotel or the somewhat larger Fortingall Hotel.

Major Ramsay strives to give his guests a superior degree of comfort and elegance, which is also reflected in the menu. Food, wines, and spirits are included.

What To Take

The hunting period is one week of which five days are devoted to hunting and the sixth day is an alternate in case of weather. At Farleyer House, guests change for dinner and a similar practice is followed in the hotels. On the shoot, it is important to be comfortable and not too visible. Dark clothing and a hat are recommended. It is frequently wet underfoot and you should have waterproof boots. Rain gear is also in order and it can get chilly, so you should have an extra sweater or jacket.

Two shotguns are preferable to one and most sportsmen prefer 12 gauge side by sides. Over and unders are used, but are less common. You may also use 16 or 20 gauge, but these are also not as prevalent as the 12's. Ammunition is supplied, but you may want to bring your own, at least for starters.

Cost

The cost of a week at Farleyer is approximately $1,500 for the hunter and about $400 for the non-hunting wife or guest. The charge covers almost all aspects of the accommodations and shooting. Each gun is provided with a loader who will look after him and his equipment. The loader will also carry the extra shotgun, ammunition, and rainwear or heavier clothing.

If you would like more information, write or call Adventures Unlimited.

DRIVEN PARTRIDGE SHOOTING IN SPAIN

Increasing numbers of American sportsmen have been traveling to central Spain each fall to match their shooting skill against the remarkable Castilian partridge. More commonly known as the Red Leg, this cousin of the Chukar flies higher, farther, and faster than the Chukar and is an extremely difficult target in the rugged terrain in which it is hunted.

Shooting in the best partridge areas is done by driving (each drive or beat is called an "ojeo") similar to the drives for grouse on the Scottish moors. The flight of each bird varies considerably with weather and terrain and provides some of the fastest shooting found anywhere.

On a calm day, the birds may come in low, skimming over rocky ridges and plunging down gullies in a swerving glide. With a wind blowing, they will pass overhead, drifting in the air current. At times, you may be in a ravine where you can see the birds approaching at high speed in their downward flight. More likely, you will be below the brow of a ridge and the birds appear suddenly over the skyline, leaving only seconds to shoulder the shotgun.

The unique aspect of this shooting is the use of two guns, preferably a matched pair. Only two shells are permitted in each gun (even with pumps or autoloaders). Newcomers to this type of shooting average one partridge for five shells. It's even more difficult when coveys of 8 to 20 birds approach at the same time. You simply cannot

Shooting Blind, Spain

day. Mid-October through mid-January constitutes the partridge season in Spain.

Spanish hunting party

What To Take

Each hunter should be equipped with a pair of double barreled shotguns. Twelve gauge is the standard and probably the wisest choice. You may bring your own shells and also purchase good ammunition locally at current market prices.

Weather may vary within a week from warm and sunny to cold and wet. You'll need warm clothing, rain gear, and waterproof boots. The hotels, of course, are typically European and it is customary to dress for dinner.

Accommodations

Guests are accommodated at the elegant Parador de Tourismo in Toledo. The atmosphere is typically Spanish and the town of Toledo is a fascinating attraction to visit.

Cost

Shooting fees are charged at the rate of $750 per week, but do not include tips to loaders and spotters, because it is the custom in Spain for each gun to offer the tip personally. The rates at the Parador are $120 for the six-day stay (double occupancy) and include meals, the transportation to and from the hunting grounds, boot cleaning, gun cleaning, tips to the hotel staff, and tips for the drivers in the field.

waste a second in deciding which bird to shoot first or you'll be turning around to get a shot off. Veterans of this type of shooting get off the first two rounds as soon as the birds are within range. Then, they take the second shotgun and get two more shots. In the interim, the secretario (the colorful Castilian equivalent of a loader) has reloaded the first gun and there may be a chance for two more shots behind the line.

Most of the organized shooting takes place in the areas of Toledo and LaMancha at about 2500 feet above sea level. A day's shooting consists of five or six drives over 1500 acres and possibly 2000 acres. Thirty to fifty beaters are used depending on the terrain. A beat will normally be used twice a year and daily bags run from 200 to 1200 birds.

Concealment, of course, is all-important and both guns and secretarios are stationed behind blinds made up of foliage or bushes at about sixty yard intervals. Positions are drawn each day and provide an equitable system of rotation throughout the

Water Fowl

"Hot on the Scent"

JAMES BAY, CANADA

Wingshooting on the shores of James Bay is a memorable and unique experience. It is here that ducks and geese gather before heading south in front of the advancing winter. Thousands of birds wheel over the expanse of marshes and it is fantastic to listen to the Cree Indian guides literally talk the birds down.

Blue and snow geese predominate in this area, but a quarter of the geese are Canadas, offering a perfect mixed bag. You can add ducks to the picture with pintails, mallards, and blacks in greatest number. There is also a mixture of shovelers, whistlers, bluebills, blue and green-winged teal, and Wilson's snipe.

The hunting is done on the western shores of James Bay near historic Fort Albany on the Albany River. It's a 250-mile charter flight from the jumping off point at Timmins, Ontario over unbroken forest and then colorful muskeg until the plane follows the shoreline of James Bay.

Accommodations

Sleeping quarters are modest, but comfortable. You're pretty far north in an area where the winters are long and the visitors few. Food, of course, is plain, but nourishing and filling. There's a guide for each two hunters and a cook back at camp.

What To Take

You can leave your city clothing back in the city. This is hunting country and warm clothing is the most important consideration.

You'll need long underwear, hip boots, walking boots, a warm parka, a waterproof parka, and heavy trousers. Don't forget that they should all be drab colors on the outside. And, pack a flashlight along with your other personal items.

It's important to bring your own shotgun and shells. There is ammunition for 12 gauge and 16 gauge shotguns at camp, but you would be wise to rely on this for emergency use. The gauge, of course, is personal preference, but unless you are an experienced wingshooter, you would do best with 12 gauge.

Cost

The trip is five days from Timmins to Fort Albany and return and includes everything but ammunition and personal items. The season is from mid-September to mid-October. Cost is $325 for the five days.

For further information: Adventures Unlimited.

CLUB DE PATOS, YUCATAN

If you've shivered in a duck blind on a frosty morning with cold rain pelting you in the face and the dampness seeping through every layer of clothing, you will enjoy the warmth of duck hunting at Mexico's famed Club de Patos. Located on the west coast of the Yucatan Peninsula near Merida, Club de Patos offers outstanding waterfowl shooting on a 50 square mile lagoon which teems with thousands of birds from all four U.S. flyways.

All shooting is done from blinds over decoys, and once the decoys are placed, the hunter can anticipate a uniquely thrilling duck hunt. There are more than ample opportunities to bag your limit and you can choose your shots. Being selective also gives you the option of using lighter gauges if you prefer. There's plenty of time to wait for shots at closer range.

Pintails, teal, and widgeon are most common in the Club's hunting area, but there are seven other species of duck in sufficient number to insure a rewarding hunt. Mexico's liberal game laws are honored at all times and they generally permit about 15 ducks daily and 20 ducks on weekends.

Exceptionally good quail hunting is also available either as an afternoon option after waterfowl shooting or in place of waterfowl in the morning. You can expect about 20 coveys of birds in the morning and from 8 to 12 coveys in the late afternoon. All quail shooting is done over pointers.

Club de Patos also offers skeet shooting, tours of world famous Mayan ruins, and can even arrange for you to do some tarpon fishing in the lagoon. Combining tarpon fishing with wingshooting is an ideal way to make the most of your stay.

Permits and Gun Rentals

To hunt at Club de Patos, you need a valid Mexican hunting license which will be obtained for you at a cost of $25. The importation of guns into Mexico is not difficult, but anyone importing firearms must have a gun permit.

The cost of the permit is $18, but it takes a minimum of 30 days to get one issued, because several government agencies must handle this form. If you prefer to bring your own shotguns, the Club will help you obtain the form, but you must start the procedure preferably a couple of months in advance.

The rental rate for a shotgun at Club de Patos is $5. Both 12 gauge and 20 gauge are available and the Club has Winchester Model 101 over and unders plus Remington 1100's (auto loaders).

What To Take

Life at Club de Patos is informal and relaxing. For waterfowl hunting, you will need lightweight hunting clothes plus a warm jacket or sweater. The Club furnishes hipboots and rain gear when necessary, but if you wear a particularly large size boot, you may want to bring your own. Slacks and shirts are perfect for wear around the Club in the evening. Don't forget a bathing suit. And, if you plan to go quail shooting, you'll need a good pair of boots, because the terrain is extremely rocky and difficult to walk in.

Whether you take your own shotguns is a matter of personal choice. You may, however, bring your own shells. Shells are also available at the Club at approximately $5.00 per box for heavy load, plastic shells, and less for others. The Club normally stocks Remington 12 gauge, 16 gauge, and 20 gauge in both heavy and field loads, but they could be out of stock in a particular shell.

Accommodations

The Club is a 40 minute drive from Merida and is serviced daily by jet. You will be met at the airport, assisted through customs, and chauffered to the Club. Guest accommodations include handsome, comfortable rooms with private baths. There is a swimming pool, a beach, and a skeet range plus a lounge for social activities. The food is excellent and the dining room features a blend of American and Mexican cuisine with game and seafood specialties.

Cost

The price of the hunting package at Club de Patos includes land transportation, the complete hunt each morning for ducks or quail, meals, accommodation, and packaging of game to take home. Price is $325 per hunter for three days and four nights. Non-hunters are billed at the rate of $105 for the three days. In addition, afternoon quail hunts are available at a cost of $25 and a tour of Mayan ruins is $30 per person.

For further information contact Adventures Unlimited or Fish and Game Frontiers. Or you may write direct to

Club de Patos
Att: Robert A. Crawford
5075 Rosell Road, NE Suite 118
Atlanta, Georgia 30342

COLOMBIAN DOVE AND DUCK HUNTING

The average U.S. dove shooter or waterfowl hunter finds it difficult to visualize the hordes of birds available to hunters in certain areas of nearby Colombia. The sky is often black with birds. In the Cauca Valley near Cali, for example, doves are so numerous that they pose problems to crop production in the valuable grain fields. In Colombia, there are no daily limits and the local farmers urge hunters to take as many birds as possible.

On the northern coast of Colombia near Barranquilla, there are marshes teeming with thousands of blue-winged teal. No one need tell you the challenge offered by teal, and in Colombia they just keep flying and flying and flying.

To combine dove hunting with waterfowl, there's a package tour that provides for three days of dove hunting and three days for waterfowl over a nine day period. A minimum party of four is required for this trip and the maximum is eight hunters.

What To Take

The temperature in Colombia can be extremely warm during the day and it can average 70 degrees at 3,000 feet where much of the dove shooting takes place. Lightweight clothing is the answer and a camouflage outfit is perfect. Make sure you have long-sleeved shirts and long trousers plus a peaked hat. Tennis shoes or other lightweight footwear is ideal for both types of shooting. You'll need a sport jacket and slacks for traveling and for the better hotels

in Colombia. Daily laundry service is available, which helps cut down on clothing.

There are going to be insects, especially near the marshes, so you should have a good repellent and rubber bands or tape to close the ankles and cuffs on your clothing.

Shooting glasses are always a good bet from a safety standpoint and they should have yellow lenses for cloudy days and darker lenses for those times when the sun is bright. Ear plugs are another must because you'll go through hundreds of rounds of ammunition if your shoulder can take it. You may also want to bring a pair of shotguns so you can switch when one gun gets hot or as a replacement in the event of a malfunction.

The choice of shotguns is always a personal item. If you want to shoot at everything within 45 or 50 yards, take your 12 gauge. Doves fly at both close and long range. Ducks are hunted over decoys, but there is plenty of close pass shooting. You'll have opportunity to use 20 gauge and, if you enjoy it, even the .410. Don't forget gun cleaning equipment and a can of rust-preventative lubricant.

You can start off with your own shotgun shells, but will have to supplement your supply with either American shells, or Colombian shells (which are excellent). American shells are about $6 per box, while the local brands are about $5 per box. It's not uncommon to use six to twelve boxes per day.

Accommodations

Lodging is at comfortable, clean hotels noted for their fine foods. Guides are efficient, friendly, and speak English. Safe and comfortable vehicles are used to transport you to the hunting area. You'll be in the care of professional operators who act as your hosts with a spirit of hospitality and concern for your well-being.

Cost

The combination dove and duck hunting adventure operates between November and March and the nine-day wingshooting package is $750 per person. Air transportation is extra.

For information on this exciting trip contact your travel agent, Fish and Game Frontiers, or write

Colombian Hunting
Mr. Alberto Lleras
Calle 71, No. 5-10
Apartado Aereo 3444
Bogota, Columbia

Additional Dove Hunting Trips in Colombia

There are other excellent outfitters in Colombia that specialize in dove hunting and we would be remiss not to mention one or two more. All hunt basically the same area near Cali and lodging is in first class hotels in that picturesque Colombian city. You are transported daily to the hunting areas. If you prefer, one outfitter will set up a tent camp for you at no extra charge. Shotguns and shells can be rented locally if you happen to be passing through the area.

Information and bookings for these additional trips can be handled through Adventure Associates.

If you are in Colombia, we recommend Huntours, Ltda., Apartado Aereo 2392, Cali, Colombia (Phone: 62-14-45) or Equatorial Outfitters, Box 548, Popayan, Colombia (Phone: 21-86).

Big Game

THE FULL AFRICAN SAFARI

Every hunter has heard tales and read story after story about going "on safari." Back in the early days, it took a long time to even reach the African continent by ship and then work one's way inland to the better hunting areas. The sportsman of that era frequently devoted three months or more to the total trip.

Today, everything has changed but the hunting. Modern jet aircraft span the globe with incredible speed and, once you arrive in Africa, charter aircraft take you to the camp of your choice.

A full African safari is still the experience of one's lifetime and, unless you've been on one, no writer can fully convey the significance of this adventure. Suffice it to say that once you have been on safari, you will want to return again and again.

Traditionally, most safaris were operated in East Africa, because this was the dividing line between northern and southern species of game. Hunting is still good in East Africa, but the trend has been toward safaris in Southern Africa in such countries as Mozambique, Angola, Botswana, and Zambia. There has also been a move to the north for different species of game and the Sudan is perhaps the newest safari country.

Typically, the full safari encompasses 28 to 30 days. This varies somewhat with the area hunted and the species you seek.

Some outfitters will book a hunt as short as 15 days, while most set 21 days as a minimum. Where the hunter seeks to collect certain rarer or more difficult trophies, the safari may run 35 days. The time is necessary to search for trophies, since it isn't a question of merely taking a representative sample of a given species.

In southern Africa, most hunting takes place during the winter months which would correspond to our summer. That's the dry season and the animals are more congregated. For planning purposes, the season starts in April or May and continues through October.

Although you can often book your own safari directly, it is generally best to use a travel specialist who is intimately familiar with the various types of safaris offered and can advise you on a number of matters. A quality travel consultant can make the planning of your trip much easier and there is no cost for the service. Keep in mind that areas change and outfitters sometimes change. You may have a friend who hunted with someone a few years ago and had an excellent hunt. Things may still be perfect with that outfitter and his area. On the other hand, there may be changes and there may be better opportunities for the species you seek. It is important to check out a safari program and get the latest information.

There are many competent (and famous) safari outfitters in Africa.

To give you a "feel" for a safari, let's look more closely, for example, at the Safariland Concession along the Save River in Mozambique. Under the direction of Baron Werner von Alvesleben, Camp Zinave has been established as the main headquarters. Werner is one of Africa's colorful characters and has lived and hunted in the bush for 35 years of his life. The natives know him as Munjunjonjo (the tall one) and he is the kind who gains your respect as a conservationist and professional hunter.

Mozambique offers some of the finest opportunities for hunting in Africa today and the heart of the game country lies along the Save River. Hunting is permitted north of the River, but Werner, with the encouragement of the government, has established a game preserve where only cameras are permitted south of the Save.

A well-organized safari is a mobile operation that moves you and your equipment to the game areas. From Zinave, you would probably move out to one or more of the satellite camps. These are tent camps of a semi-permanent nature and are strategically located to coincide with game patterns. For certain species, mobile tent camps may be established. You would be using four-wheel vehicles with no restrictions on the mileage. The goal would be to help you collect trophies.

With you would be the gunbearers, trackers, skinners, drivers, cooks, field and camp assistants, and your professional hunter.

Each country has its restrictions on the number and caliber of firearms you may bring in. In some places, .22 caliber is not permitted, but otherwise, choosing the correct

Greater Kudu, Mozambique

rifles is a matter of personal choice. It is possible to rent firearms if you notify the operator in advance, but they would prefer you to bring your own so that you are familiar with them. You should have a light, medium, and heavy caliber rifle, plus a shotgun for waterfowl and upland birds. The light rifle for plains game might be a .270 Winchester, .300 Weatherby, or a similar caliber. For buffalo, lion, and large antelope, you will probably use a .375 or .378. If you were limited to a single rifle, this would be the one to take, fitted with a 4X scope or a variable scope. For thick-skinned game, you would need a .400 caliber or over, such as a .458 Winchester or .460 Weatherby.

Remember that even though you are on a hunting safari, you can still capture the rare moments on film. There will be plenty of game to photograph. A good 35mm single-lens reflex camera with built-in exposure meter is the answer and you should have it fitted with a telephoto lens as well as a normal lens. Take a pair of binoculars for game viewing. These should be seven or eight power (7 x 35, 8 x 30, etc.). Higher powers are difficult to use unless you are stationary and sometimes the vibration of a vehicle with the motor running (out of gear) is enough to make viewing difficult with nine or ten power glasses.

The costs of safaris vary, but we can offer some general guidelines. Figure it will cost between $7,000 and $11,000 for a 30-day safari with one professional hunter. Trophy fees will be added to this, plus the cost of preparing and shipping your trophies to the taxidermist. You can bring the cost down by sharing a professional hunter with another member of your party. Air transportation is extra. These are average costs; you can buy some safaris for a little less and a few will cost you more.

If you are interested in more information on the African experience, contact either of these outdoor travel specialists:

Fish and Game Frontiers or Adventures Unlimited

THE AFRICAN SHORT HUNT

The African Short Hunt is an intriguing adventure in southern Africa that takes you to two of the most storied hunting areas for a limited amount of time, at a cost that is comparable to a hunt in North America. Designed for the businessman who cannot be away from his office for longer than perhaps ten working days, the Short Hunt enables the sportsman to take a wide variety of species.

Southern Africa is like East Africa was forty years ago—unspoiled and unexploited. This vast area comprising 2.3 million square miles has only 1/10th the number of visitors that East Africa has. Not only is there plenty of elbow room, there is an abundant supply of game as well.

The keynote of the Short Hunt is quality, and your hunt is first class in every respect. The program combines the resources of two of Southern Africa's finest safari companies: Basie Maartens Safaris in Southwest Africa and Safarilandia in Mozambique.

To keep the cost down, two hunters share the same professional hunter, which merely means that your professional works twice as hard, because he's just as anxious for you to get your trophies as you are. In Mozambique, you will hunt the Cape buffalo, the highly prized nyala, impala and other species. Southwest Africa offers the greater kudu, giant gemsbok (oryx), mountain zebra and others.

You will experience a true miniature safari and the only difference from a full safari is the amount of time spent.

Accommodations

The thrill of any African hunt is going on safari with mobile tent camps set up along the way. This is the way Basie Maartens operates, moving the camp to the best areas. Tents are specially designed and the sleeper tents have attached bathrooms. There is also a dining tent. Food is top quality and usually supplemented with wild game for the main course; a meal never tastes better than it does outdoors.

At Camp Zinave, the names of hunters who have been there before you decorate the white walls and you may add your name before you depart. You will probably also spend time in the field camps which are permanent tents located in the quality hunting areas.

What To Take

You won't need quantities of clothing on safari, because laundry is done almost daily. Basic safari clothing is an excellent choice. Khaki trousers and shirts that can be laundered and are permanent press make things easy. Footwear can either be desert boots (ankle high) or low bird shooters' boots.

The Short Hunt operates during Africa's winter when rainfall is at a minimum and animals are concentrated near waterholes. In spite of the movies you may have seen, it can get cold, especially in early morning. From May through August, you'll need warm clothing in Southwest Africa and a warm jacket will be valuable in Mozambique as well. Lightweight down is the perfect choice and you should also have a hat and sunglasses. Shooting glasses for the early morning will also help.

You may bring your own rifles and ammunition for this hunt. However, firearms are included in the price at Camp Zinave and you can rent guns in Southwest Africa for perhaps $30 or $35. It's also worthwhile to bring a shotgun (or rent one there), since there is upland game shooting if you have the time. Gun calibers reflect personal preference, but you should use .270, .300, or 7mm magnum for most shooting and a .375 for heavier work.

Cost

The price of this African Short Hunt is $2,937 based on two clients using the services of one professional hunter and includes all costs except airfare, trophy fees in Southwest Africa, gratuities, alcohol, items of a personal nature, and the rental of firearms.

For further information contact *Fish and Game Frontiers.*

As increased business activity takes more and more Americans to the Near East, it should be remembered that "short hunts" can be arranged in African wilds which are not many hours flying time from Rome, Athens, Beirut and Cairo. Details regarding these opportunities can be obtained from Adventures Unlimited.

Grizzly Bear

MIXED BAG IN ALASKA

The Alaska Range reaches from the Alaska-Yukon border westward to McKinley Park, then south to Lake Illlamina, the largest lake in Alaska. Mt. McKinley, the tallest mountain in this hemisphere, rises majestically above the Alaska Range until it tops out at 20,300 feet.

Clark Engle's camps nestle south and west of the park about 15 miles from the boundary. Dall ram, grizzly, black bear, moose, caribou, wolf, and wolverine are found in abundance in this wilderness area. Clark's many years of successful guiding and outfitting in these mountains have confirmed that this area is exceptional, because it is relatively inaccessible and because game species move in and out of McKinley Park where hunting is not permitted.

Sheep camps have been established at the headwaters of the Tonzona River and Pinkston Creek. They are accessible by aircraft, but it takes an extremely experienced bush pilot to put a plane down in that country. The fall season starts in late August and continues until the middle of November.

A four-wheel-drive rig is used to set up spike camps and for bringing back meat, capes, and antlers. Aircraft are only used for transportation from main camps to spike camps and back again. Clark Engle is not only a master hunter, but a dedicated sportsman and emphatically insists that aircraft will never be used to hunt, circle, or harass game at *any* of his camps.

There is a minimum of ten days required for any one hunt, but you may book for as long a period as you desire, providing you do it in advance. Reservations must be for a specified number of days and extensions are not possible because they would infringe on the time scheduled for other hunters.

Dall sheep, Alaska Range

Accommodations

This is wilderness country, but the hunting camps are excellent. The 10 x 12 sleeping tents are erected on a log frame with wooden floors, built-in beds, and plenty of firewood for the stoves. The cook tent is 16 x 20 on a frame which not only furnishes plenty of room for a meal, but provides a place to drink coffee and swap hunting yarns in the evening.

It is important that you arrive in Anchorage early. Remember that weather can be a factor and it is vital that you arrive at the hunting camp the day before your hunt is scheduled to begin. You have the option of arriving even earlier, but you must make reservations in advance so that lodging can be set up for you.

Reservations will be made for you at the hotel in Anchorage and the airport limousine will be available to transport you there.

The Seasons	
Sheep	August 10th to September 20th
Caribou	August 10th to March 31st
Moose	August 20th to December 31st
Grizzley	September 1st to October 15th
Brown Bear	October 1st to October 31st
Black Bear	No Closed Season
Wolf	September 1st to April 30th
Wolverine	September 1st to March 31st

Physical Condition

This is rugged country and the success of your hunt often depends on your physical condition and ability to walk through this terrain. In booking a hunt, your age and an honest appraisal of your physical condition should be mentioned so that the hunt can be better tailored to your needs. Before coming to Alaska, you should start a program of physical conditioning such as jogging, push ups, and climbing, if possible. If you work in an office building, consider walking up and down the stairs each day. You'll find that pre-conditioning will make the hunt more enjoyable for you and you'll return home happy instead of exhausted.

What To Take

To hunt this area, you need functional clothing that is well broken-in and field-tested. This is not the place to discover that a pair of trousers chafe or a jacket binds

under the arms. If you hunt in September or October, you need extra clothing to keep you warm and your rifle and cameras should be winterized. Above all, you will need a heavy down jacket, long underwear, and three or four pairs of warm mittens. Insulated shoe packs or boots are also vital for that time of year.

On most of the earlier hunts, a specialized type of hip boots are worn and it is suggested that you buy these in Anchorage when you arrive. Unlike fishermen's boots which are loose at the ankles, these are tight fitting and hug the ankles closely. If you wear an odd size or large size, you might check their availability in Anchorage in advance.

The rifle, of course, is a matter of personal choice and it should fit the game species you seek. Scopes should be sighted in before you arrive. It's also wise to carry a lightweight pair of binoculars with you and rain gear.

Cost

A ten day, mixed-bag hunt costs approximately $3,000 plus licenses

and permits. The basic hunting license is $20, but tags for each species are as follows: sheep, $150; brown or grizzly bear, $150; moose, $100; black bear and goat, $75; caribou, $50; wolf, $50; and wolverine, $25.

For further information contact Adventures Unlimited.

Mountain Goat

MOUNTAIN HUNTING IN IRAN

Iran not only offers the finest mountain hunting in the world, but it is off the beaten path and you are unlikely to encounter other hunters for hundreds of square miles. In addition to the long list of game trophies available in abundance, a safari in Old Persia offers deluxe accommodations and services in the tradition of the African hunt. Iran treats its visitors hospitably and with concern and courtesy.

Persian Shikar under the direction of master hunter Massih Kia offers a variety of hunting packages that are available for less money than most good hunts in Northern Canada or Alaska, and that includes airfare. You will see more game and your chances of success are almost 100%.

Programs are offered lasting from eight to twenty-one days and, with excellent jet service, you can hunt Iran in no more time than it takes for a North American adventure. Game is unbelieveably abundant and the professional hunters are extremely competent.

In the breathtakingly beautiful Alborz Mountain country, you hunt Urial or red sheep, Persian ibex, big brown bear, the magnificent stag, huge Russian wild boar, and roe deer. There's also the option of adding a short hunt on rugged and picturesque Ghoyoundaghi Island for Armenian sheep.

The Central Alborz offer trophy ibex and red sheep and you can take two of each. Iran also has its version of the Grand Slam and

Fishing for caviar in the Caspian Sea

there is almost a guarantee that you'll accomplish the feat if you attempt it. Ibex and three species of wild sheep comprise the Grand Slam.

The hunting season in Iran lasts throughout the year for certain species, but in some areas, winter hunting is not conducted because the weather is too harsh. Temperatures vary with the season and the altitude. Snows may occur in the mountains in the late fall and winter, but hunters seldom face extreme cold. The maximum altitudes for most hunting is 6,000 to 7,000 feet or less. The only exception is in the Central Alborz where you may go to 12,000 feet. Obviously, this hunt is not offered in the winter.

Accommodations

You will be met at the airport in Teheran and transferred to a first class hotel with a la carte meals included. Lodging in the hunting area will be in comfortable stone hunting lodges, nearby best available hotels, or, infrequently, safari tents. This, of course, depends on where you hunt and the species mix you desire.

Services in the field include a competent English-speaking professional hunter, four-wheel-drive vehicle, and a full safari staff that consists of a driver, waiter, cook, game skinner, game wardens, and field workers. Good mountain saddle horses with horse handlers are provided for your comfort in most hunting locations.

Food is always the best available and can even include caviar fresh from the Caspian Sea. Vodka, wines, beers, and soft drinks are also provided.

What To Take

For most hunting in Iran, flat-shooting rifles are recommended with a good scope (2-7 variable with fine reticle is a perfect choice). Many shots will be fairly long range. The best calibers would be .270 Winchester, 7mm Remington magnum, .308 Winchester, .264 Magnum, .300 Magnum plus a number of special big game calibers by Weatherby or other custom rifle makers. Calibers under .243, automatic, or semi-automatic weapons are not permitted in Iran.

A total of 100 rounds of ammunition for each caliber may be taken into the country. Lightweight binoculars and a camera or two are well worthwhile and, if you have a spotting scope, take it along.

Clothing will depend on the time of year you hunt and the area you are in. Walking boots can be any type that you find comfortable for rugged hunting at home. For mountain hunting, you'll find boots with Vibram lug soles a good choice, but there are some visitors who still prefer their "bird shooters" or rubber pacs.

Camouflage or drab colored clothing is favored by Iranian hunters and wardens, because mountain game is particularly sharp-eyed. For winter hunting,

you'll need a down parka, warm hat, and gloves or mittens.

Cost

Hunts range from a low of $870 for an 8 day Urial sheep-Persian ibex hunt (April to September) to a standard of about $2,000. The Grand Slam prices out at close to $4,000. In addition, there are license fees of about $50, controlled area fees of $15 to $20 per day on hunting reserves, and trophy fees for each species taken. The trophy fees vary by area hunted and the size of the trophy. Other than personal items, everything else is included in the package price except for international air transportation.

For further information about this trip, contact your travel agent, or Fish and Game Frontiers, or write direct to
Mr. Kamran Atabai
P.O. Box 11/1934
Teheran, Iran

ELK, BEAR, AND MULE DEER IN WYOMING

Appealing because of the majestic splendor of its mountains and enhanced by the tranquility of its remote location, the northwest corner of Wyoming above the 2.5-million-acre Shoshone National Forest and east of famed Yellowstone National Park offers some of the most superb big game hunting in the West. Elk, bear, mule deer, sheep, and a few mountain goats share this beautiful habitat with upland game birds and an equal abundance of small animals.

The K Bar Z Ranch is an oasis in this otherwise wild countryside that is laced with clear mountain streams that harbor four species of trout. It's paradise for any serious big game hunter and a challenge to the hunter who is anxious to test his skills.

Hunting takes place in an assigned territory within the heartland of the Absaroka Wilderness Area. It's a half day's ride to either of the two well-situated hunting camps. You'll have a licensed guide with you, wranglers to handle the horses, and all the necessary camping facilities will be provided for a comfortable and rewarding hunt.

Accommodations

Built of native lodgepole pine to blend into the wilderness setting, the clean and relaxing cabins at the K Bar Z are spaced to provide maximum privacy. Your cabin has modern bathroom facilities and there is plenty of hot water. The open, wood burning fireplace is both rustic and functional, and there is always an ample supply of seasoned wood.

Meals are served at the main lodge with the traditional style of the Old West, tailored to tempt the tastebuds and in sufficient quantity to satisfy even the cavernous appetite of a growing boy.

The Ranch maintains a string of top saddle and pack horses for hunting, fishing, packing back into the mountains.

What to Take

Nestled at 7,000 feet beneath a vista of higher mountains, the K Bar Z Ranch enjoys a delightful climate the year around. During the summer months it can be cool because of the altitude and a light down sweater or jacket is perfect to ward off the chill in the evening. In the fall, the weather can get much colder and hunters should plan on taking warm clothing, a pair of well broken-in boots, and raingear. Remember that this is mountain country and the weather can change rapidly. You can always shed clothing if you have too much, but you can't put it on if you didn't pack it.

Most hunting is done with medium-caliber rifles and a good scope. The Ranch recommends .30-06, .270 or 7 mm Magnum for much of the shooting. Of course, rifle selection is personal and you may have your own favorite caliber. If you are going to be on hand when the trout season is open, you should bring your own tackle. Flyrods or light spinning outfits are ideal with a typical assortment of trout flies and lures. Waders are worthwhile if you take your fishing seriously, but if you

merely want to wet a line, you can get by without them, providing, of course, you use spinning tackle and don't need room for a backcast. Some hunting trips require the use of spike camps or camping out and you may be more comfortable in your own sleeping bag and air mattress. The Ranch can give you this information once you decide on what you prefer to hunt.

Cost

The K Bar Z Ranch bases its hunting packages on ten days duration and the cost is approximately $100 per day. A ten day hunt for elk, moose, mule deer, or grizzly is priced at $1,000; while the cost is $1,200 for sheep or mountain goat. These rates include all meals and lodging, saddle horses, your guide and wranglers, and most incidentals. License fees, ammunition, the rental of guns, and similar personal expenses are billed separately.

Licenses

The State of Wyoming employs a lottery or drawing system in issuing non-resident big game hunting licenses. The names are pulled out of the hat early in the year and the fortunate hunters are notified so they can make arrangements. If you plan to hunt Wyoming, you can obtain full details on this license drawing by writing to the Wyoming Game and Fish Department, Box 1589, Cheyenne, Wyoming 82001. They'll send you a copy of the *Wyoming Hunting Bulletin* which provides a schedule of fees, seasons, and other information.

For more information on the K Bar Z Ranch, contact Adventures Unlimited.

TAHR AND CHAMOIS IN NEW ZEALAND

Finding no native game in New Zealand, early European settlers introduced a wide variety of species from all over the world. Heading the list is the tahr, one of the world's rare game species that inhabits the Himalayas. New Zealand is the only place where a sportsman will see them in real numbers.

The chamois comes from the Alps, but, like all of the mountain animals introduced, the chamois is more plentiful in New Zealand than in its original homeland. All of these game animals have adapted so well that antler and horn growth is superior.

New Zealand offers a number of deer species starting with the red stag from the forests of Europe and including the fallow deer from Europe, sika deer from Manchuria, rusa deer from Java, Sambar deer from Ceylon, and the native American whitetail.

With no limits or closed seasons on game animals in New Zealand, hunting is undertaken the year around. February through October, however, is best for deer because they are carrying their racks at that time. Tahr and chamois are best during high summer or in the snows of winter. Deer are in rut from March to May and this would be the absolutely best time. Your guide will even imitate the roar of the stag.

Accommodations

After your arrival at Christchurch Airport, you will be met and transferred to Lilybank Lodge by fast station wagon. Lilybank is headquarters for New Zealand Trophy Guide Service, Ltd. and nestles on a tree-sheltered knoll above the confluence of the Godley and MacCauley Rivers. On three sides, snow peaks rise to 9,300 feet and this is the place where tahr, chamois, and red deer abound.

The Lodge has four twin bedrooms with separate bath and toilet facilities. It is centrally heated, electrically serviced, and designed for maximum relaxation for sportsmen and their wives. Meals feature unique New Zealand recipes for fish and game, topped off with New Zealand wines and cheeses.

Horses and four wheel drive vehicles are used to transport you to the hunting areas. New Zealand Trophy Guide Service also offers longer safaris for a number of game species in addition to tahr, chamois, and red deer. The safari may cover 1,000 miles or more and you will be transported by any means necessary to get you to the game areas the quickest.

What To Take

All caliber rifles in the .270, 7mm, .30-06, .308, and .300 magnum range are suitable for New Zealand hunting. Calibers smaller than .270 are too light and anything over .300 magnum are too heavy. Handguns are illegal. If it is inconvenient for you to bring your own rifle, New Zealand Trophy

Guide Service will supply a rifle and scope at no extra charge.

New Zealand is below the equator and the seasons are reversed. When it is summer in the northern hemisphere, it is winter down there. Clothing should be of the mountain hunting type such as you might use in British Columbia. In spring (October-November) and fall (February-March), you may need a few items of light clothing.

Boots are of paramount importance and they should be a good quality leather with deep-treaded rubber soles. The guides wear tricounis on their boots which are iron cleats fastened to the edges of each sole. They can be

fitted to your boots on request.

Drab colored clothing for hunting is still the best choice.

Cost

The minimum hunt is ten days and the charge is $100 per day for one hunter with one professional guide. If two hunters share the same guide, the cost is reduced to $75 per hunter per day. There is a special helicopter safari guaranteed to get you tahr, chamois, and red deer in a two to four day period. Cost for this safari is $1,100 per person.

For further information contact Adventures Unlimited.

Tahr, Southern Alps, New Zealand

On Firearms

PREPARING FOR YOUR HUNT

Hunting is a personal experience and everyone approaches it differently. Most serious hunters, however, want to reap maximum benefit in the outdoors and do everything possible to insure a successful hunt. They know from experience that if one is properly prepared and conditioned, the hunt will take on even more meaning and will be that much more rewarding.

Preparation starts with conditioning. Nothing is more miserable in the field than to discover you are out of shape for the hunt or that an item of equipment fails you at an inopportune moment. Even a walk across level fields can be taxing for someone who sits behind a desk everyday and then comes home at night and flops in an easy chair. The problems compound as you move into mountainous country and the stalk can take hours of hard work after spending days searching for the trophy. If you can't get into position for a shot, the hunt may turn into a failure.

Hunting situations are available throughout the year in some part of the world and, although you may be in shape during your own hunting season, you could have to undergo some special conditioning in the off season. Jogging, bicycle riding, and walking up and down flights of stairs all help to strengthen the leg muscles and build stamina. If you work in a tall

" . . . if you want to score consistently, it takes practice."

office building, try going up and down the stairs to your office. Some hunters utilize a nearby football or baseball stadium for their exercise, jogging up and down the rows of seats.

Clothing is another area of concern. Perhaps your feet haven't been in a pair of boots in months. Long before you set out on your hunt, start wearing your boots for a portion of each day. And if you're going to exercise by climbing stairs or making use of the aisles in a stadium, wear your boots. Blisters in the field can be disasterous. Obviously, if you purchase a new pair of boots, they should be worn around your home and wherever possible almost daily until they are well broken in and comfortable.

In addition to your footwear, check

the other items of clothing. If you have to slip a light down sweater under your hunting coat, can you move your arms or shoulder a gun? New hunting pants should also be worn so that you can check them for chafing or binding. If they are washable, they should probably be washed a couple of times. Each piece of clothing and equipment should be checked out carefully long before the day of departure on a major hunt. This will not only add to your pleasure in preparing for the adventure, but it will make things run smoothly once you get there.

Every guide and professional hunter will normally work exceptionally hard for their clients. However, they are just as human as the next fellow. If they know you are in condition and that you can make the tough shot if need be, you'll find that they will add an extra measure of effort on your behalf. If, after a long stalk, your shot doesn't even come close, or after finding covey after covey of birds you can't pick out one bird and hit it, the guide will probably try to work you into easier territory and lesser trophies.

To shoot well, you must have the right equipment and you must practice. Even the best shots in the world can't pick up a firearm after a rest of several months and expect to be in top form. It takes practice and the time to work out is *before* you embark on your hunt. Once you are in the field, it's too late.

When your hunting involves a rifle, check out the sights and the scope to make sure they are aligned and accurate. Scopes should be bore-sighted and you should fire a number of rounds to confirm that the gun is "on" and that you know how it shoots. When you arrive at the hunting camp, you should fire a few more rounds before ever going into the field to make certain that the alignment hasn't changed. This will also give you renewed confidence on the spot that you can hit a target.

Shotgunners should get in plenty of practice sessions on the trap or skeet field before going wingshooting. It will help to sharpen your eye and build your confidence. However, don't make the mistake that many shooters do when practicing on a trap or skeet field. They become concerned with their scores and would be embarrassed in front of others to show poorly. Actually, the best practice comes from shooting skeet

from the international position where the shotgun is held in the basic field position rather than shouldered. You might try the same approach for trap, although it is much more difficult.

Preparation is the key to success. Anyone can get lucky, but if you want to score consistently, it takes practice.

TRAVELING WITH FIREARMS

Although thousands of people travel to every area of the world for sport hunting, it is becoming increasingly difficult to transport firearms. The rash of recent hijackings and the political situations in some countries make the sportsmen subject to more careful scrutiny. Many people, including airline personnel, frequently do not understand firearms for legitimate purposes and their reactions can be quite emotional.

The first object to keep in mind is that you have the responsibility of getting your shotgun or rifle to the hunting area in undamaged condition and on time. All of the outdoor travel specialists are familiar with the requirements and take great pains to help their clients minimize the inconvenience.

There used to be a time when all you had to do was put your firearm in a soft case or saddle scabbard and carry it aboard. Normally, it would be placed in the cockpit for you and you could pick it up as you deplaned. With rare exceptions, those days are over. Realistically, the last thing you

want in some places is to be seen with a firearm in your hands. One can never tell what the reaction will be any more.

For that reason, the best means of transporting rifles and shotguns are in rigid, foam-lined cases. There are a fair selection of these on the market and they generally cost between $25 and $100, depending on the one you select. Firearms today are normally shipped in the baggage compartment of the aircraft and the only way to prevent heavier items from crushing the contents of your case is to buy an impact-resistant case. A few airlines might have special shipping containers which they will give you or rent to you, but it's not worth taking the chance when you arrive at the airport.

Your rigid firearms case should be locked, but it should not be sealed in such a way that it can't be opened for inspection. In this country, the ticket agent is required to inspect the firearm to insure it is unloaded. If it is a rifle and the bolt can be removed, he may ask you to do so, so it is best to handle this in advance. Pack the bolt carefully and put it in your suitcase. Some travelers carry a roll of tape in a carry-on bag and then tape the gun case after the inspection.

The best way to carry ammunition is in the original boxes from the manufacturer. Pack these in your suitcase with adequate padding. Federal regulations prevent you from carrying ammunition loose. It must be in boxes with partitions between each round or with an inner box fitting in an outer box.

If you are traveling outside the United States, you should be aware of the requirements in each country you visit. They vary and your outfitter or travel consultant should have the latest regulations.

It's important to realize that guns shipped as baggage are insured by the carrier at the same rate as any other baggage. This would be limited to a total of $500 in the United States and about $9 per pound in international travel. Your guns may be worth a lot more than that and it's best to purchase additional insurance from the airlines or from your insurance agent before you travel.

Anyone traveling with firearms will need more time to check in, so it makes sense to arrive at the airport somewhat earlier than you usually would. Make sure that your name and address is written on the hard case or attached to it on a tag. You should have the make, model, caliber, serial number, and other information about your firearms in your wallet.

With some outfitters, it is recommended that you ship your guns in advance consigned to them. If you follow this procedure, do so far enough in advance so that the outfitter can tell you by letter or cable that the guns have arrived.

When you arrive at your destination, pick up your gun case as soon as possible. In remote areas where flights continue onward, it's a good policy to watch for your case coming off the airplane. If you don't see it, have someone check before the plane takes off.

At your earliest opportunity, unpack the firearms and inspect them for signs of physical damage. All damage should be reported to the airline immediately. If you have a rifle with a scope, it makes sense to fire a test round or two before you embark on your hunt. The scope may have been aligned before you left home, but you should make sure it is still aligned before you put the crosshairs on your target.

We all recognize that airlines are doing their best to get your baggage, your firearms, and you to your destination at the same time and without damage. Most are willing to cooperate with you any way that they can, but some caution on your part can often make the difference.

As with other personal articles of value, guns should be registered with U.S. Customs — using number stamped on gun — before leaving the United States. Registration form can then be produced when you return through U.S. Customs assuring unquestioned clearance.

NOTATIONS

THE OUTDOOR ADVENTURE

Sasafari—An African Experience
Iceland, Faroe Islands, and Greenland
Greenland Dog Sledging Expeditions
Alaska—The 49th State
In Search of Ancient Mysteries
Galapagos Islands—Crossroads of Evolution
The Mighty Amazon
Jungle River Adventure, Brazil
Himalayan Trek in Nepal

Coping With Climate

SASAFARI — AN AFRICAN EXPERIENCE

Sasafari combines the wildlife highlights of several countries of southern Africa in a carefully tailored, single itinerary.

Focusing on Rhodesia, Botswana, Mozambique, and South Africa, Sasafari utilizes a fleet of private aircraft and a few commercial flights to eliminate uncomfortable and unproductive travel time between the best game-viewing area. The three-week program, which permits stops in Europe, covers 3,000 miles in Africa over a period of 19 days—3,000 miles where most tourists have never traveled.

Sasafari is one of the outstanding game-viewing and photographic programs available in Africa today because it concentrates on the unspoiled, unexploited, and unvisited parts of southern Africa. You stay at some of the most famous and storied African lodges and camps, some of which were only available to full hunting safaris and most of which can only be reached by charter aircraft (there are no roads and no scheduled flights).

Equally important, in a number of areas you ride in Land Rovers or other open vehicles driven by professionals and you are permitted to leave the vehicles in many of the places. You get a different feel of Africa in the open than you do from the interior of an air-conditioned vehicle that merely drives through a region.

A highlight of the Sasafari program is the exclusive participation in the Save Basin Research Project at

Camp Zinave in Mozambique. You will see professional hunters and biologists immobilize big game with drug darts for the purposes of scientific data recovery. The opportunities for close-up photographs of these animals is unparalleled and it is equally exciting to watch the animal recover and move off after the antidote has been administered.

Sasafari spans the area from the famed Okavango Swamp and the

legendary Khwai River Lodge in Botswana that Ruark and Hemingway made famous to Victoria Falls, the Zambezi River, and the game-laden middle ground of Mozambique and South Africa. Once you have seen the different areas, you can appreciate how the various habitats attract different species of animals and birds.

The viewing season is from late March through the end of October each year, which coincides with fall, winter, and early spring in Africa. This is the dry season and as water becomes less abundant, the animals concentrate near the water holes, making them easier to locate and view or photograph. Each group is also escorted by a competent hostess who is extremely knowledgeable about the animals, people, and places you will visit.

Accommodations

Sasafari is a first-class experience. In Johannesburg, you stay at the plush President Hotel; at Victoria Falls, your accommodations are at the historic Victoria Falls Hotel; at other stops you stay at the finest hotels and lodges available.

What To Take

With the exception of the Victoria Falls Hotel where it is customary to dress for dinner in the evening, all of the lodges are informal. During the day, bush clothing or sportswear that is comfortable is a must. Because of the space limitations on the private aircraft you will be flying, each participant is given a special suitcase designed to fit in the planes' luggage compartments. It is requested that you keep your baggage to a maximum of 35 pounds.

In addition to your clothing, you will need a good pair of binoculars, camera equipment, and, if you are interested in bird life, a good field guide. For those who enjoy capturing the live sound of the outdoors, a tape recorder would be valuable. You will also want to use it to record native music and the

exciting chants of native dancers. You can't believe how the ground can shake when these dancers stamp their bare feet in unison.

Cost

The three-week Sasafari costs approximately $2,000 per person in a group of seven or more plus international airfare from the United States to Africa and return. Air transportation within Africa is part of the package.

For more information contact your travel agent, or Frontiers International. Or write

Sasafari
P.O. Box 10418
Johannesburg
Rep. of South Africa

ICELAND, FAROE ISLANDS, AND GREENLAND

Following the path of the ancient Norseman, Viking Air Safaris has combined the scenic, geological, and naturalistic glories of these northern paradises with the flavor of their histories and people. It is a unique opportunity to enter the outdoor world of active volcanoes, geysers, snow-capped mountains, sparkling salmon rivers, lush green valleys, and strange lava formations.

Iceland is virtually treeless, yet the tundra vegetation is refreshingly green and attractive. There's always something to see, and the flocks of Icelandic sheep add charm to the countryside. Icelandic ponies seem to be everywhere in this colorful land.

The Faroe Islands offer a world of soft green hills, charming fishing villages, majestic mountains, and sea vistas that fill the mind's eye with many memorable pictures. If you elect to take the option to Greenland, you are in an Arctic wonderland of iceberg-choked fjords, glaciers, and foreboding mountains, behind which lies a permanent ice pack.

The climate along the Icelandic coast is mild because Iceland is surrounded by the Western Ocean Drift, an extension of the Gulf Stream. Though daytime temperatures in the summer are quite mild, the weather is very changeable because of the strong ocean influence. Rain squalls can come and go with disconcerting speed and strong winds are not unusual. And since the country borders on the Arctic Circle, there is practically no real darkness in the middle of summer.

Hot springs abound, and these thermal regions are worth a visit to view the steaming sulphur banks, boiling mud, hot springs, and roaring steam cracks, some of which are harnessed for industrial use. Near Lake Myvatn, in Northern Iceland, where the famed Laxa i Aldaldal River is born, there are caves where you can go swimming in pleasantly warm water either winter or summer.

There are over 230 distinct species of birds that have been observed in Iceland, 76 of which are known to nest there. It is truly a "must" excursion for the amateur ornithologist or serious bird watcher. You can expect to add a number of birds to your life list and you should be able to see such rare species in their natural habitat as the gyrfalcon, gannet, and great skua. Part of the tour includes a visit to the Westman Islands where, on Heimaey Island in 1973, there was a major volcanic eruption and a quarter of the fishing village was destroyed.

On Heimaey Island you will also be able to get close-up photographs of birds such as the puffin, guillemot, fulmar, kittiwake, and others.

The Faroe Islands lying 250 miles southeast of Iceland and halfway to Scotland has some 255 species of birds including the nesting grounds of the rare gannet.

Greenland is a unique experience and you will stay at the Arctic Hotel (if you add this option to your itinerary) in Narssarssuaq (pronounced Nar-sass-a-whack), directly across the fjord where Eric The Red first settled. It's a rugged and remote land where the Greenlanders (Eskimos) work the sea and the fields for their existence.

Accommodations

Viking Air Safaris takes pride in offering the finest accommodations available in each location. You will stay at the modern Loftleidir Hotel in Reykjavik. With the Scandinavian influence throughout this region, no one ever goes hungry at the table and the amount of food and its quality will be an experience.

What To Take

This is primarily a viewing and photographic safari. Whether you use a Kodak Instamatic or highly

sophisticated cameras, bring your equipment with you and enough film to capture the beauty of this world on film. Even if you haven't become addicted to bird watching, you will enjoy having a pair of lightweight binoculars with you. And, it is quite possible that before the trip is over, you will have begun your own life list of birds.

Summer temperatures in Iceland vary between 45 degrees and 75 degrees, and you could run the range three times in one day. In the better restaurants of Reykjavik, dress is fairly formal, but the rest of the trip is much more informal. Clothing should be comfortable and you should be able to dress in layers so you can adjust to temperature changes quickly.

You'll find that a pair of lightweight, slip-on overshoes such as the calf-length Totes can be an important addition to your wardrobe. You can slip them over your shoes for walking where it might be muddy or wet, and they can make things comfortable if it

should rain. A rainsuit would also be valuable.

If you go to Greenland, you should have heavier clothing available, because it can get cold very suddenly.

What To Buy

Iceland and the Faroe Islands are known for their woolen goods. Some are handmade and others are factory produced, but all are beautiful and are sold much cheaper than you would find them in the United States. Most woolen goods in Iceland are not dyed (some are in the Faroe Islands) and some of the natural oil from the sheep remains in the wool, adding a waterproof quality to it.

If you've always wanted a sheepskin (the kind that goes on the floor for a rug), Iceland is the place to get one. They range in price from $12 to $20, but they are bulky and you should leave some room to pack them in your suitcase.

There are typical souvenirs in Iceland and the Faroe Islands, plus an array of pottery, gold, and silver.

Cost

Including international airfare from New York to Reykjavik and return, the cost of the Viking Air Safari to Iceland and the Faroe Islands is under $2,200 for a 15-day tour. The option to Greenland involves 5 days and 4 nights and would be priced at $300 per person. This includes airfare from Iceland, hotel, tours, and all meals except dinners.

Wings In Iceland

The primary purpose of "Wings In Iceland" is to help you identify as many species of birds as possible and add them to your life list. It is also tailored toward bird photography. The itinerary has been specially designed to visit every type of habitat and utilize air transportation between major areas to minimize time spent in traveling. You should be able to identify between 70 and 100 species of birds including several that are very rare.

This is a ten-day excursion with accommodations at the best hotels, air transportation between major areas, and an itinerary tailored for the naturalist. The cost is approximately $1,350 including air transportation from New York to Reykjavik and return.

Frontiers International has all the necessary information along with departure dates.

GREENLAND DOG SLEDGING EXPEDITIONS

There are some travelers who not only want to see different ways of life, but they want to take part in it. It is for this type of person with an adventurous spirit that the Greenland dog sledging expedition was designed. You have to be in robust physical and mental condition to be accepted as a member of the group and allowed to participate, but if you do go, your outlook on life may never be the same.

Under the leadership of British Major Mike Banks, one of the world's leading Arctic explorers and member of 11 major expeditions, you will live in Greenland for two weeks just as the Eskimos do. The program is designed to acquaint you with dog sledging and camping out in the Arctic winter. Trips are scheduled from mid-March to late April when the main thrust of winter is over, but you may still have to sit out a blizzard in a tent or help push a dog sled through deep snow.

If you agree to participate in this adventure, you must understand two things before you embark. First, you are not a spectator, but a participant. That means that you must be ready to lend a hand in all activities from pitching tents to carrying ration boxes. Secondly, you must agree to abide by

decisions made by Major Banks, which are based on his years of experience and always consider the interest and safety of all party members.

Your adventure starts in Reykjavik, Iceland and, after a chance to adjust to the time zone and do a little sightseeing, you move across the Denmark Strait in a charter aircraft and land at Kulusuk, a small island off the east coast of Greenland. A helicopter takes you the short distance to the mainland and the village of Angmagssalik. There is a tiny hotel where you will spend three nights, while the days are devoted to becoming familiar with Arctic conditions and dog sleds.

The helicopter will return after three days and ferry you about a

half hour up the fjord to the settlement of Kungmiut from where you will operate for the next ten days. Accommodations are in private houses when you are not camping out.

The first phase of this operation is to learn to camp out in specially designed, expedition tents under Arctic conditions, something that few campers in the world have ever experienced. Once you get the feel of camping and dog sledding, the key phase of the program begins. You will make several trips of two or three days duration, exploring the various parts of this beautiful fjord country.

The climate in eastern Greenland is dry and cold, with temperatures at this time of year moderating to perhaps 15 degrees above zero, but hovering right around zero. You can expect a proportion of sunny days, but you must also be prepared for snow and blizzard conditions accompanied by strong winds.

Your outfitter will supply you with a parka and Arctic-type sleeping bags. However, you will be required to bring the remainder of the warm clothing you might need. Full details will be made available if you are accepted.

The cost of this 19-day Greenland Dog Sledging Expedition is $2,195 per person from Reykjavik to Reykjavik. Air fare from New York to Reykjavik and return is not included, but runs about $290.

More information is available from Hanns Ebensten Travel, 55 West 42nd St., New York, N.Y. 10036. Telephone: 212-354-6634.

ALASKA - THE 49th STATE

Alaska is a wilderness land that beckons to many, because it is the last frontier of the United States where nature in all its beauty and hugeness is still unfolding. The possibilities for viewing wildlife firsthand are tremendous and the spectacular scenery is a photographer's dream. There are countless touring programs to every region of Alaska and you can find something to interest you every month of the year. Here are just a few to excite you.

Alaskan Safaris

From the oil fields at Prudhoe Bay to Mt. McKinley National Park to a week-long boat trip through the untold islands in southeastern Alaska, Alaska Safaris will custom tailor a trip specifically to your needs and tastes. Whether your interest is in bird watching, wildlife photography, or scenic viewing, the itinerary is carefully planned for your traveling pleasure.

Since these safaris are created for the individual group, meaningful costs cannot be quoted until the itinerary is developed. You can get full particulars from Frontiers International.

Alaskan Photo Hunts

Under the direction of Clark Engle, Alaskan Photo Hunts are for the professional or serious amateur photographer who wants to take pictures of wild game and spectacular scenery. Clark is one of Alaska's top professional hunters and he uses his hunting knowledge and spike camps to put the photographer on his quarry.

Photo hunts are conducted in Mt. McKinley National Park and at McNeil River Brown Bear Reserve. Hunting with firearms is forbidden in both of these areas. The McNeil River Reserve offers the best opportunity to capture the huge brown bear on film. The brown bear is the largest carnivorous land animal in the world. From a cave near a waterfall, you can watch these bears feed on salmon and perform in the wilderness. These are completely wild bears in a totally remote area and it's wildlife photography at its best. There are also other animals to photograph on these trips.

The trip to McNeil River is seven days and starts in mid-July. A week to ten days in Mt. McKinley Park will give you a chance to see Dall rams, grizzly, black bear, moose, caribou, wolf, and possibly wolverine.

Adventures Unlimited will be delighted to send you more particulars.

Pribilof Seal Islands and Rookeries

The Pribilof Islands have long been the breeding grounds for the Pacific fur seal, and the islands are totally inhabited by these animals when they come back to mate each year. You can hear the roaring bulls for miles as they fight for their harems.

Located in the Bering Sea some 250 miles north of the Fox Island group of the Aleutian Chain, they include St. Paul, St. George, and the Otter Islands. Reeve Aleutian Airways offers three-day, four-day, and six-day tours of the Pribilofs with departures from Anchorage.

From May through September there are over one million seals on these islands and you can get close enough to make the photographs of a lifetime.

There is mch more to see than the seals. More than 180 species of birds have been identified on these islands and bird watchers from all over the world come to see these creatures and photograph them. Without climbing or exertion, you can photograph nesting birds at particularly close range. Some species are only found here and others are here in greater quantities than anywhere else in the world.

Finally, there are the 400 Aleuts who live in the community and the stories of sealing, the tundra, and the volcanic origin of these islands.

Tours run through June, July, and August and include round trip air transportation from Anchorage (2,000 miles), hotel and guides. They do not include meals. A three-day, two-night trip is $279; four-days, three-nights are $299; and the six-day adventure is $349.

Space is generally limited and reservations should be made well in advance through your travel agent or Reeve Aleutian Airways, P.O. Box 559, Anchorage, Alaska 99510.

A Final Touch

The Division of Tourism (State of Alaska, Juneau 99801) publishes a 32-page booklet entitled "Off Beat Alaska" that lists a number of places accessible only by air or water. It's worth writing for if you are searching out the unusual trip on your own.

IN SEARCH OF ANCIENT MYSTERIES

Responding to Erich Von Daniken's best selling book, *Chariots of the Gods*, Braniff International has established a conducted group tour to some of the world's most famous archaeological sites in Peru, Colombia, and Bolivia. You will explore and photograph these mysteries and share in the details that surround them, and only you alone can formulate answers to these puzzling questions.

Outside of La Paz, Bolivia near Tiahuanaco, there are ruins that some think are the birthplace of all cultures. A huge sculpture known as the Gate of the Sun stands 10 feet high, 16 feet wide, and was carved out of a single block estimated to weigh 10 tons. The Great Idol is here. This gigantic sculpture with its hundreds of superbly carved symbols has been identified as a calendar that may be 27,000 years old. It accurately supplies astronomical seasons and positions of the moon for every hour. If you can tell the world who carved it, how it was carved, and why, you can solve this mystery.

Journeying across Lake Titicaca, the highest navigable lake in the world on a hydrofoil, you will see the famous Indian reed boats that were identical to the ones used by Thor Heyerdahl for his trip across the Atlantic. At Cuzco in Peru, you will see the place where the Inca Empire of 25 million people was ruled without benefit of a written language. How did this advanced culture communicate? Nearby is Machu Picchu, so well-hidden that

it was never mentioned in history and discovered by accident in 1911. It is one of the best preserved Inca cities and it appears that people just left it. There was no natural catastrophe. Why?

The famous Nazca Plain stretches along the southwest coast of Peru. When you fly over the plain, you will see astonishing markings. Gigantic lines are laid out with geometric perfection, paralleling and intersecting one another. Some are surrounded by trapezoidal shapes and scientists tell us that these lines were laid out according to astronomical calculations. Stranger still are the mysterious and gigantic drawings or tracings on the plain in the shapes of spiders, monkeys, and birds. No one has yet been able to determine why they were made and no one has been able to explain why the Incas ran their coastal road directly through these lines. That coastal road, by the way, is uniformly 24-feet-wide with a two-foot collar on each side. In the days before the wheel or heavy draft animals, why would any culture need 24-foot roads?

Not far from Nazca on the high red cliffs that back the Bay of Pisco, a figure nearly 820-feet-high is clearly visible from a boat or low-flying airplane. It resembles a trident or candelabra and points directly to the drawings at Nazca. Von Daniken suggests that it may have been a directional marker for visitors from another planet.

In Colombia, they have begun digging up 100-square-miles of ruins at San Agustin. Over 300 stone figures have been discovered including some that are 16-feet tall. Mysteriously, the only other place in the world this type of figure is found is on Easter Island.

These special archaeological tours encompass 16 days in three countries and cost $679 per person (double occupancy) plus airfare. You can learn more about them from your travel agent or Braniff International.

GALAPAGOS ISLANDS-CROSSROADS OF EVOLUTION

Straddling the equator some 600 miles west of Ecuador and spanning some 40,000 square miles of the Pacific Ocean, the Galapagos Islands are actually the tops of gigantic volcanoes which rise some 7,000 to 10,000 feet above the ocean floor. There are 15 main islands and perhaps 50 smaller ones.

It was here in 1853 that Charles Darwin, serving as a naturalist aboard the British ship HMS *Beagle,* found animals and plants that had evolved in special ways because of their isolation. Even today, the same evidence of evolution is apparent in the flora and fauna that prompted Darwin to write *"The Origin of Species"*.

The animals and birds of the Galapagos developed in the absence of any large predators and have absolutely no fear of man. Because the animals are unconcerned with humans, photographers discover they can get amazing close-ups without using long telephoto lenses. Bird watchers are constantly excited over the 89 species that inhabit these islands, 77 of which are found nowhere else on earth. Heading the list are the Galapagos penguin, Galapagos albatross, and flightless cormorant.

Except for the sea turtles, all of the reptiles on the islands are found only in the Galapagos. The giant tortoise is reported to live 400 years. There's the non-poisonous Galapagos snake that reaches four feet in length. The land iguana is

the nearest thing to a dragon you'll ever see, feeding on cactus and reaching a length of four feet. The marine iguana lives on the lava rocks of the shore and is an excellent swimmer. Seaweed is its primary food.

Anyone who has been to the Galapagos invariably will tell you that no matter how long you spend in this idyllic, natural setting, there isn't enough time to see everything. Two motor vessels, the *Floriana* and *Iguana,* ply the waters around these islands and serve as your hotel. There are no accommodations on any of the islands for visitors. Visitors fly from Guayaquil to the main island of Baltra and then board the ships for the inter-island cruise. Normally, the ship cruises during the night so that it is at another island early in the morning. Days are spent ashore.

Although these cruises operate all year, space is necessarily limited.

Only about 5,000 visitors are able to see the Galapagos each year and, when you consider that they come from all over the world, that isn't very many people. Reservations should be made as early as possible for this once-in-a-lifetime experience. The M/V *Iguana* also makes a certain number of cruises each year from the mainland of Ecuador.

The warmest, clearest season for visiting the Galapagos runs from December to June. July through November is the coolest time of the year. Even though the islands are on the equator, they are not oven-hot, because they benefit from the cooling breezes off the cold Humbolt Current.

Comfortable, lightweight clothing is the right choice at any time of the year. For viewing and photographing on the islands, you'll want tough outdoor wear such as khaki or denim. Footwear is a matter of personal choice.

Many visitors prefer the solid hiking shoes with rubbber or cleated soles worn by backpackers. They give good support and the soles will grip any type of terrain. Others are content to wear sneakers or low boat shoes.

Aboard ship, casual sport clothing is best. You should have a sweater or jacket because it cools off on the water every evening. Space is limited on the cruise ships and guests are advised to take a minimum amount of clothing with them. If you are on an extended South American vacation, or if you have a number of city type clothes with you, facilities are available in Guayaquil to store your belongings until you return.

Island tours are conducted by trained and extremely knowledgeable naturalists. After dinner aboard ship every evening, the naturalists will give you a detailed briefing of what you can expect to see the next day and tell you what to look for. There is also time for discussion of the day's events.

There are four, five, and eight-day cruises of the islands. The length of each tour determines how many islands you will stop at. Aboard the *Floriana*, prices vary with the location of your cabin, but range from $335 to $390 for a four-day cruise, including air transportation to and from the mainland. It's $400 to $485 for the five-day cruise, including air transportation to and from the mainland. It's $400 to $485 for the five-day cruise, and the eight-day cruise is priced at $565 to $700.

The Galapagos Islands offer excellent swimming and skin diving. The fishing potential is fantastic, but hardly explored.

Detailed information and bookings are available from Adventure Associates. If you are in Ecuador, you can book the trip through

Metropolitan Touring
P.O. Box 2542
Quito, Ecuador
Telephone: 524-400

THE MIGHTY AMAZON

When Francisco de Orellana discovered the Amazon almost 435 years ago, he called it the River Sea and noted with awe that unless one saw it one could never imagine it. Starting high in the Andes, the Amazon drops 16,000 feet in its first 600 miles and then only drops 700 feet in the next 3,500 miles. Ocean going vessels can sail more than 2,500 miles up river to the city of Iquitos, Peru. Although the depth of this river can vary as much as 50 feet, it is deep enough in places to engulf a 10-story-building. And, at Leticia, Colombia some 2,300 miles upstream, the main river is more than two miles wide. There are more than 50,000 miles of waterways and 1,100 major tributaries in the Amazon Basin, accounting for one-fifth of the world's total fresh water. As Orellana said, "You have to see it to believe it."

The Amazon River Cruise was established to enable travelers to observe life along the river and taste the encompassing jungle while maintaining the comforts and safety of modern cities. A 140-foot yacht (renamed the *Amazon Queen*) now plies the waters between Iquitos, Peru and Leticia, Colombia. The yacht leaves Iquitos every Sunday and departs Leticia for the return upriver every Wednesday. On the downriver trip, you have the option of overnighting at one of the lodges along the river or you can remain aboard the yacht. On the upriver run, guests sleep aboard the yacht.

This magnificent craft is pure luxury with air conditioning

throughout, two interior lounges, and plenty of deck space to walk around. Meals are served buffet style and, in addition to American dishes, feature foods and specialities of Colombia, Peru, and the Amazon region.

The River is not only a way of life, but it is the only link between Indian tribes and river people. You will stop each day to explore points of interest on shore and then continue your cruise. There will be time to walk in the mighty Amazonian jungle and to see and photograph Indians from various tribes. The Yaguas are particularly interesting and you will stare in amazement at their skill with the traditional blowgun. A Yagua hunter can hit a small bird in flight at perhaps 40 yards with a toothpick-thin dart that is over a foot in length. There are also Ticunas and a chance to see some Jivaros.

The basic cost of a one-way trip is $215 with sleeping accommodations aboard the boat. There is a surcharge of $30 per person for the three most spacious cabins.

Leticia, Colombia

Leticia, Colombia is a river town that sits on a tiny point of land on the banks of the Amazon, some 2,300 miles from the mouth. It is Colombia's only access to this mighty waterway. A mile downriver you are in Brazil, and the other bank of the Amazon is Peru.

Leticia is the home of Mike Tsalickis, a legendary American expatriate who not only operates a motel with a swimming pool for the visitor, but is the chief animal and fish exporter for the whole region. Mike knows the jungle and the Indians. At the moment, his main interests are capturing monkeys for medical research and tropical fish to satisy the requirements of people who enjoy an aquarium in their homes.

Mike can tell you enough stories about the jungle to keep you spellbound for days, and he can also organize a multitude of trips for you that will help you to experience life in this part of the world. He'll take you to remote Indian villages or let you collect your own tropical fish. You ask for it and Mike can produce it. He's sometimes hard to get hold of; he's that kind of a guy. If you take the Amazon Queen to Leticia, plan on staying at the motel for a few extra days, but check to see if Mike will be there. And, if you expect to board the Amazon Queen at Leticia, arrive early and let Mike Tsalickis show you around. You'll never forget the experience of walking through the jungle with two men swinging machetes in front of you.

For further information contact *Braniff Outdoor Council*
or
Adventure Associates

the Amazon Queen

the Jungle Queen

JUNGLE RIVER ADVENTURE, BRAZIL

If you relish the unusual and are willing to accept the challenge of taking a step beyond the fringes of civilization to where the totally unknown begins, this Brazilian jungle river adventure will appeal to you. Brazil's Araguaia River flows northward for more than 1,000 miles until it links with the Tocantins River and then the mighty Amazon. Most of this region is jungle and tropical rain forest where primitive tribes have yet to be discovered. The next main river system to the west is the Xingu, which is constantly the subject of television documentaries and newspaper reports of not-so-lost tribes being re-discovered.

Under the supervision of Andre V. Rakowitsch, Brazil's famed explorer-surveyor who has walked through most of this area, you have an opportunity to experience life in this part of the world. The *Jungle Queen* is a 75-foot modern boatel built on two pontoons that can navigate the central region of the Araguaia River, while providing the basic civilized comforts.

Starting at the village of Santa Terezinha in Brazil's Mato Grosso, the boatel moves 100 miles down river and back again, taking you to areas that you couldn't possibly reach any other way. The only way to reach Santa Terezinha is by scheduled VASP flights or by chartered air taxi. There are no roads.

The boatel is your headquarters and it is exciting to watch the crew secure it to a sandbar for the night and then get it underway the next morning. During the day, you use modern, outboard powered aluminum skiffs to fish, explore, sightsee, or photograph anything of interest. It's an experience you will never forget.

Andre Rakowitsch will custom tailor a trip to your needs and desires. The bird life on the Araguaia, for example, boasts over 200 species and ornithologists on these trips have positively identified 150 species. There are plenty of hoatzins in the area (the bird closest to pre-historic flying reptiles), jabiru, and wood storks. Spoonbills are abundant and there are eight species of herons.

Fishing these jungle waters is a unique experience. Tucunare (peacock bass), the prime species, are extremely plentiful. In addition, you'll catch a dozen species you never knew existed. And, if you're looking for unusual sport, try fly fishing for piranha. They'll destroy flies and popping bugs with their razor sharp teeth.

Watching the Indian life along the river and listening to Andre tell you story after story about the various tribes in the region makes our Old West seem tame. The principal tribe in this stretch is the Caraja, but there are Tapirapes, Caipos, and others. These people live as primitively as their ancestors and they will often come with their dugouts to visit you aboard the boatel, willing to trade their handicrafts for items from the civilized world. The best bartering items, by the way, are clothing, fishing tackle, flashlights, pocket knives, and items that they can use in their fight to exist with nature. Beads, cheap jewelry, and similar things don't have much trading value.

The expedition on the Araguaia is well-organized and perfectly safe, but self-sufficiency is the survival ingredient. The boatel operates on

this theory and carries plenty of spare parts for the motors and other equipment to make any necessary repairs. You must also bring everything you need.

On the other hand, although things normally run smoothly, there could be changes to the itinerary or minor inconveniences. A motor could break down and it will take time to fix. Possibly, the plane doesn't come in on time and you'll have to wait. Planned food supplies may not arrive and substitutions may be made. This is a completely isolated region and you should recognize that fact. That's precisely what makes the trip so unusual and exciting, because it has been totally untouched by visitors. The area exists as it always has.

Meals on the boatel are wholesome and interesting. Main dishes include meat and also locally caught fish. They are designed to conform to the tastes of the American or European visitor, but you may get a chance to sample some local delicacies as

a side dish. Andre may even let you taste caiman (alligator) and its flavor will surprise you.

The tour operates during the dry season from May to October, which is winter in that part of the world. There may be a shower or two during this time span, but rains are infrequent and the river continues to drop daily until it reaches its lowest point in October. During the course of the year, the river will rise and fall 25 feet or more. Temperatures during the day hover between 80 to 90 degrees, but the evenings are cooler. May and June are the coolest months and October about the warmest.

Insects are not a problem, but you should take some repellent with you anyway along with an anti-histamine cream of some type. Clothing should be comfortable and designed for tropical, outdoor situations. Andre recommends that you bring well-worn clothing so that you can leave some of it behind if you choose and use the room in your luggage to pack out artifacts that you may have obtained from the Indians.

The cost of this unusual experience is $420 for the week (Sunday to Saturday), plus air transportation from Rio de Janeiro. It's an adventure you will never forget and when you read about another tribe discovered in the Xingu reserve, you'll know you were there.

For more information, contact Adventures Associate or write

Andre Rakowitsch
Matagoias Company
P.O. Box 568
Goiana, Brazil

HIMALAYAN TREK IN NEPAL

Nepal is a land of contrast with towering mountains and steaming jungles. The adventurous Himalayan Trek in Nepal begins with a trek on foot in the Annapurna region of the Himalayas, where you will reach 9,500 feet before starting down again. Then, there's explorations of the Terai jungle on elephant back, and a canoe trip on the Rapti River which has never been available to the traveler before.

This trek is led by Lute Jerstad, a native of Oregon who was one of five Americans to climb Mt. Everest and has climbed Mt. Rainier more than 60 times. He is equally at

home in Nepal and insists on enjoying the beauties of that country at an unhurried pace.

Along with your Sherpa guides, you will walk about seven miles the first day at an altitude of 2,800 feet to the village of Hyengja and spend the night under canvas. Throughout the tour you will have spectacular views of many of the famous Himalayan peaks including the Annapurnas and Machapuchare. Over the days, you work your way to the 9,500-foot level, enjoy the scenery, take photographs and then work back down.

A short flight takes you back to Katmandu where you have a chance to spend a night in a hotel and then you're on your way to the Terai jungle via another short flight. Wildlife in the jungles is plentiful and unusual and on this trip, you should see a Bengal tiger and some leopards in addition to other creatures.

After two days on elephant back, you'll welcome the chance to climb aboard a raft or dugout canoe and make your way back on the Rapti River.

The mountain country will be cool in the evenings and sometimes cold, but the jungles will be very warm all the time. To insure that you have the correct clothing and best equipment, the outfitter will provide you with a duffel bag, rucksack, parka, water bottle, flashlight, knife, down pants, and wind pants. You will be instructed on what else to bring. Keep in mind that this is not a trip for the timid or for those who are not in reasonably good physical shape. It is not an endurance test, but you have to be able to walk and climb to negotiate the first part of the trip.

The cost of this fantastic and varied outdoor adventure is $1,900 for three and a half weeks in Nepal, not including international airfare. If you would like to know more about it, contact

Hanns Ebensten Travel

COPING WITH CLIMATE

You may not be able to change the weather at the moment, but you can certainly do something about it. Modern outdoor clothing coupled with an expanded knowledge of the outdoor environment make it a relatively simple matter for any sportsman to remain comfortable from the Arctic to the Equator. Mental attitude is the key. If you can learn to dress for the weather without wasting energy trying to fight rain or cold or heat, you'll reap a far greater measure of enjoyment from your main outdoor pursuits. Let your selection of clothing handle the elements.

The place to start is with a good quality rainsuit. Unless you are planning to hike across a desert, you can bet that sooner or later it will rain, or that you might be aboard a boat where wind-blown spray will have the same effect. It's often better to buy a rainsuit that is a size larger than you would normally take. There are several reasons. The larger size will fit easily over a heavy parka if you happen to be in a cold climate. And it is easier to get on and off, especially when it is wet.

In buying a rainsuit, make sure the one you choose has a hood on the parka and that the parka, itself, extends down far enough to cover any jacket you might be wearing. In a strong rain, it's hard to keep all of the water out, but some rainsuits do a better job of it than others. If you choose a model with a full zipper down the front of the parka, make sure there is a waterproof flap that folds over the zipper. Otherwise, water will leak through the zipper. If you are going to

use the rainsuit near salt water, the zipper should be nylon or a non-corrosive metal.

Most rainsuit pants tie at the waist. Check the method of tying for ease of operation. Also, it's a good idea to measure the length. If your trouser or slack legs extend beyond the rainsuit, you know they will get wet. When you try on the suit, sit down and make sure the pants legs don't ride up above your cuffs. Finally, check the closures around the hood on the parka and consider the weight of the whole suit. Lightweight suits are easier to transport and less bulky, but if you plan to do a lot of walking through brush, the lighter materials may not be as sturdy.

Experienced outdoorsmen learn to pack for any eventuality and never assume that the weather will be as perfect as the travel brochures might predict. An average temperature of 60 degrees can mean a low of 40 degrees and a high of 80 degrees. Seasoned practitioners adhere to the adage that you can always shed clothing, but you can't put it on if you don't have it with you. For that reason, it is best to plan for extremes and you'll never be caught short.

Perhaps the most valuable item of outdoor clothing is a lightweight, down-insulated jacket (often called a down sweater). Jackets of this type can be crammed into a very small stuff bag and packed easily. You can wear your down sweater aboard a boat early in the morning to ward off the chill until the sun climbs above the horizon. It's equally great for adding warmth under a heavier down jacket or for wearing around camp. And, no matter where you travel, you have

some protection against any form of unexpected low temperatures.

Outdoor clothing should be simple and functional. High style items are best left for city wear. Winter or summer, clothing should be relatively loose and should fit without binding or constriction. The trick, of course, is to dress in layers so that you can adjust to temperature fluctuations quickly and with a minimum of effort.

To dress properly in the outdoor environment, it's important to have a passing knowledge of how our bodies function to keep us warm or cool. It's been said that if you want to keep your feet warm, put your hat on. The reason is that our heads are the main radiators for getting rid of excess body heat. Our bodies have built-in thermostats that send the heat to our torsos first, so that our vital organs are kept at the proper temperature. To do this, the blood supply to our extremities (hands and feet) is reduced. However, the body must continue to send adequate blood to the brain, so there is no reduction in heat carried to the head.

Once the torso and head have adequate heat, our bodies send the excess to the surface of our skin and then the extremities. Cooling is handled mainly through perspiration and by allowing heat to escape from the torso. That's where loose fitting, open-collared clothing makes a difference in warm weather and the same principle can be used to keep you from perspiring in winter.

When the weather gets cold, perspiration can cause problems. During any 24-hour period, the body normally gives up 1½ pints of water through the skin (in addition to any perspiration). Moisture in clothing is a problem and one of the most important ways of keeping warm is to let it escape without soaking into clothing

If you allow for an air space between your body and the first main layer of clothing, you can keep the clothing from absorbing the moisture. This is best accomplished with the new "fishnet" type of underwear that has a mesh with openings at least ⅜'s of an inch or more. Depending on how cold it is, you can wear regular clothing or insulated underwear on top of the "fishnet".

As you dress in layers, keep in mind that there should be some way to open the clothing to allow warmth to escape and thus prevent perspiration from forming. You can do this by tossing the hood back on a parka and perhaps opening the neck area. Two-way zippers help to eliminate heat from the torso area and, if you are wearing insulated pants or a snowmobile suit, the zippers on the legs help you to ventilate quickly. Look for these features when you purchase outdoor garments.

Keeping warm is also a matter of insulation in the clothing we wear and insulation is measured by the thickness of the dead air space. The colder the temperature, the thicker the insulation needed to keep warm. The best materials are lightweight, compress very easily, are washable, will breathe and allow moisture to escape, and are resilient. Goose down has been the prime material fulfilling these requirements, but there are also some excellent synthetic substitutes. Remember that

warmth comes with the thickness. A two-inch thick down jacket has four times the insulating qualities of a half-inch thick down jacket. And there are no miracle materials to compensate for thickness.

In cold weather, it's important to wear a hat to prevent heat loss and a hat is equally vital in warm climates to protect you from the sun. On the water, a broad-brimmed hat over polarized sunglasses helps you to see better. And, for some reason, in equatorial climates, a hat helps to ward off sunstroke or heat exhaustion.

As your travels take you closer to the Equator, you must be more aware of the sun and its effects. Obviously, loose clothing is going to feel a lot cooler and it allows moisture to escape. Our present day permanent press garments are the greatest thing for the traveling sportsman since the Wright Brothers made their famous flight. You will find that the greater the cotton content in permanent press clothing, the better it will absorb perspiration. In our experience, clothing with less than 35% cotton can become a bit uncomfortable in sticky weather.

Keep in mind that temperatures are relative. Even in the tropics, you might need a jacket if you're on the water at daybreak. The sun, of course, can be devastating once it burns through the early morning haze and you should recognize that the rays are stronger nearer to the Equator.

Those people who spend great amounts of time in the outdoors try to protect their skin from the ravages of the sun. A tan might look nice, but extensive exposure is a known way to contract skin

cancer. For those of us who only face a strong sun during vacation time, the problem isn't as acute. However, you can get a nice tan and partially protect your skin at the same time by following a few simple precautions.

Somewhere among your gear should be a bottle or two of a sunscreen lotion. Sunscreens are designed to block out the majority of ultra-violet rays of the sun—the rays that tan our bodies and also burn our skin.

If you're going to be on the water, remember that the reflection of the sun from the water's surface can be devastating. Veterans may wear a short-sleeved shirt, but few will wear shorts or expose any part of the back or chest to the sun. For one thing, it seems to drain some of one's strength, and for another, it can subject a person to severe sunburn. If you must get a tan, do so gradually by limited exposure each day.

Finally, don't forget that the area around your eyes is extremely sensitive to the sun and your eyes should be protected from the strong glare of the sun (especially from water or snow) with polarized sunglasses. If you're going to be on the water, make sure you have an extra pair of sunglasses with you at all times. Extra sunglasses back at the lodge won't help if something happens to your original pair early in the day.

When you select your outdoor clothing, make it functional and don't forget that it is more important for your clothes to protect your body than to win fashion awards. Coping with climate is easy if you prepare in advance.

Colorado River

WOODS & WATERS

Underwater
Cayman Kai
Anthony's Key
Palau and Truk
Greek Isles
Little Dix Bay

Climbing
Bob Culp Climbing School
Dick Pownall Mountaineering School
Eastern Mountain Sports Climbing School
Exum Mt. Guide & School of American Mountaineering
Northwest Mountaineering Guide Service

Touring
American River Touring Association
Nantahala Outdoor Center
Wilderness Outfitters

Family Outings
Grand Teton National Park
VW Camping in Europe
Nature with a Naturalist
Ski Touring

Start Them Young
The Chase Ranch
Star Island Nautical School
Outward Bound
Don Kerbis Tennis Ranch

Underwater

UNDERWATER EXPLORATIONS

The mysteries, beauty, and challenges of the underwater world have lured snorklers and scuba divers beneath the surface of the sea for a variety of reasons. While some find it relaxing to explore majestic formations, and others want a closer look at the various types of coral, all underwater enthusiasts demand good visibility and relatively warm water to add the ultimate to their sport.

Because it is an individual experience enjoyed with others, diving appeals to outdoor people of virtually every age group. Once you've donned snorkel, mask, and flippers, you've entered another realm. It is only a small step forward then to scuba diving and to earning your certification.

As a requirement for participation in any scuba diving trip or adventure, you must have certification to dive. It's easy to obtain, but there are no shortcuts, since your safety and that of others diving with you depends on your competence. You may prefer to obtain certification as part of a trip or vacation to a diving resort. If you choose that method, however, remember that you will be busy learning while others are enjoying the attractions of the area.

A better method is to learn scuba diving before you go. Courses by qualified instructors are given in most towns and cities across the country. Many are free and others are available at minimum charge. If there is a diving club in your area, any of the members can tell you where to learn. The local YMCA or YWCA usually offers courses from time to time, and they could certainly tell you where diving instruction is being given.

There are also special diving classes held throughout the year in many of the larger cities. In New York, for example, Walt Hendrick runs a 45-hour, eight-week course at the Chalet Club for groups of 15 at a cost of $110. If you think you would prefer one-to-one instruction, he will teach you privately. The cost for 30 hours with him is $250, with an assistant, $200.

On the West Coast, New England Divers, 11830 West Pico Boulevard, Los Angeles or 3860 Rosecrans Street, San Diego offers a 40-hour, four-week course for $65 (groups only). This should give you an idea of the time and money involved in learning scuba diving. Once you are certified, you will be a welcome member on any diving trip. Children can also be taught to scuba dive, but they should be at least 10 years old before they start.

If the primary purpose of a trip is for diving, you should place your confidence in a travel agency that specializes in diving trips. General travel agents will book any trip you request, but they do not usually have the knowledge required for a specialized sport, nor can they offer you the same caliber of group trips. Four of the leading names in scuba travel are:

*Lee Turcotte's Atlantis Safaris
P.O. Box 303
Miami Shores, Fla. 33153
Tel: 305-754-7480*

*Walt Hendrick at the Chalet Club
135 East 55th Street
New York, New York 10022
Tel: 212-758-8669*

*Dewey Bergman and Carl Roessler
at See & Sea Travel Service
680 Beach Street Suite 340
Wharfside, San Francisco,
CA 94109
Tel: 415-771-0077*

*Dr. Mort Walker, Dive Tour Leader
484 High Ridge Road
Stamford, CT 06905
Tel: 203-322-1551*

Group travel opportunities offer the best deals in terms of money and often in terms of learning more about the sport. These tours are led by experienced divers who can teach you a great deal on the spot and also help enrich your underwater experience. Equally important, airlines usually make concessions to groups and your equipment is often included without charges for overweight.

Just about every resort in the world that caters to the serious diver will supply air tanks, weightbelts, backpacks, and air. However, it's a good idea to double check this before you walk aboard a plane and take off for distant parts. On the other hand, you should pack your own regulator, gauges, mask, snorkel, and fins. These are best carried in a bag that will fit under the airplane seat and should be part of your hand luggage. Your wet suit can be packed in a suitcase. If, for some reason, you do have to take your own tank, you might phone the airline in advance and see if they cannot provide some type of protective packaging for it during transit.

The number of exciting underwater explorations are increasing constantly. The ones we describe below are some of the finest and most unusual trips known at this time. If you have developed a specialty such as exploring wrecks, working underwater caves, shell collecting, or merely fish watching, you might make this known when you request more information.

Cayman Kai Scubaventure

Although jet planes touch down on its paved runway daily, Grand Cayman Island in the British West Indies is a remote and perfect blend of sea and sand some 475 miles from Miami where the scuba diving and snorkeling can best be described as fantastic. Three sides of the island are protected by coral reefs and on the north side, the sea drops away from 55 feet to more than a mile, forming the famed Cayman Trench.

At the moment, there are some two dozen different dive sites, each with a distinctive characteristic. Some boast sunken wrecks; others have underwater caves, chimneys, and coral walls; and rare black coral juts from the face of the Cayman Trench. The water is superbly clear and the diving opportunities rank with any in the world. It is a spot that caters to and welcomes divers.

Cayman Kai is a casual resort where you can kick off your shoes and enjoy life at your own pace. You won't need ties or jackets for dinner, but you will need a pair of old tennis shoes for beachcombing or walking on the coral reefs. Tanks, backpacks, weightbelts, and air are furnished, but it is best to bring your own life vest, regulator, gauges, snorkel, mask, and fins, even though you can rent these items at nominal cost.

Accommodations are in well-appointed sea lodges with kitchen, patio, living room, and bedrooms. You can also have the use of privately owned beach homes on a rental basis. The rate schedule depends on the options you require and whether you prepare your own meals or dine at the resort's restaurant. As a guideline, it is $45 per day per person (in groups of 10 or more) including meals, lodging, unlimited air, daily use of scuba equipment and boat, and the guidance of a diving instructor.

If you're interested, contact Dr. Mort Walker.

Anthony's Key Resort, Roatan, Honduras

Roatan Island lies 30 miles off the Honduras coast in windowpane clear water with coral reefs, tropical fish, wrecks, and the other exciting aspects of underwater explorations. You jet to Honduras from the gateway cities of New Orleans or Miami and then fly to the island aboard local air taxis from San Pedro or La Ceiba. A four-wheel drive vehicle takes you the short distance from the landing strip to the carpeted Tahitian huts at Anthony's Key Resort.

The beautiful and picturesque huts are nestled near the sea, on a hillside, and even on the nearest key. There's an open air lounge and dining room. Living is easy and relaxed. There is no need for

formal clothing. Sportswear will suffice and you'll need your diving gear. Tanks, weightbelts, and backpacks are available and you can rent the other items, but it is still best to bring your own regulator, mask, snorkel, life vest, and so forth.

Periodically, special group tours are arranged by the Chalet Club so that participants can qualify for their NAUI Intermediate Certification Card. The basic cost of a week at Anthony's Key Resort is $315 per person as part of a group. Air fare ranges between $120 and $200 from a gateway city.

Palau and Truk in Micronesia

If you have always dreamed of finding a diving spot where the number of wrecks are practically unlimited and virtually unexplored, you might want to consider the islands of Palau and Truk in the remote corners of the western Pacific. Back in 1944, the Japanese fleet was trapped in the Truk Lagoon and most of the support ships were sunk. More than 60 wrecks lie on the bottom of that lagoon just as they did on the fateful day of 1944 when they went to the bottom. Visibility is excellent and most of the vessels lie in shallow, warm water where a wreck enthusiast can have the experience of a lifetime.

At Palau, there are additional wrecks and even a Japanese Zero on the bottom, but the main attraction are the coral reefs, perhaps the most colorful in the world. At one point, there is a coral wall that starts at the surface and

drops to 2,000 feet.

Diving tours to Micronesia are operated periodically and you can get details on the next one from The Chalet Club.

Greek Isles Cruise

There are some 1400 islands strung out through the Aegean and Ionian Seas. Visibility in many areas ranges from 60 to 120 feet and, although the salinity is slightly higher than the Atlantic, the tides and currents are negligible. In addition to coral and underwater formations, many of the dives are over wrecks that date back to the earliest recollections of man. Every fall, Lee and Helen Turcotte lead twenty divers to a few islands specially chosen for their interest to the underwater explorer.

On the itinerary are famous islands such as Delos, the birthplace of Apollo, Hydra, an artist's haven and Mykonos, now a lively resort. For the diver, however, the best stops may be at Melos, where an entire sunken city waits to be explored and at Santanorini, supposedly the site of the lost city of Atlantis.

Your base will be a luxurious 100' charter vessel, and there are days set aside for visits to Athens and Rhodes. Most diving is done during the heat of the day, when it's cooler to be below, so in the late afternoons and evenings you will be free to poke around the islands and their villages. The cost per person is $800 for 17 days, including round-trip airfare. For more information, contact Atlantis Safaris.

Little Dix Bay Hotel, Virgin Gorda, British Virgin Islands

Virgin Gorda is a sunny, unspoiled island on the very edge of the Virgin Islands' archipelago. The beaches are spectacular and there are lots of secluded spots to spend a day away from everything and everybody. Best of all, underwater visibility here ranges from 70 to 100 feet in waters where the temperature never drops below 75 degrees. Just put on a snorkel or full scuba equipment and you can spend days nosing around down below, diving for conches or following the fish.

At nearby Anegada Reef, there are over 200 known shipwrecks to be explored. Bert and Jackie Kilbride, the resident scuba experts at Little Dix Bay, will be happy to arrange a trip for you, or to give help or instruction. Ask to see the wreck of the Rhone near Salt Island; Captain Cousteau once called it one of the most photogenic wrecks he has ever seen.

Little Dix Bay Hotel has been designed for minimum impact on the environment with maximum comfort for the guest. There are 66 rooms arranged in cone-topped cottages along a crescent beach, with several other outstanding beaches nearby. The food is excellent and the buffets famous. The cost for five days of scuba diving is $210. For more information, see your travel agent or contact Rockresorts, 30 Rockefeller Plaza, New York, N.Y. 10020.

Greek sponge diver

Climbing

Have you ever thought of climbing a mountain? Few sports will ever take you so far away, beyond and above it all as this one, out into crisp air and quiet forests, onto breathtaking ledges and trails, near lakes and meadows few people ever see. It is a challenging, relentless discipline which requires skill, determination and endurance, but the feelings of accomplishment which it generates are enormous and very, very real. Once you have begun you will discover that there are trips of every sort for the climber to take.

The mountaineering schools in this country are as widely scattered as the peaks they climb. The basic techniques—such as rope handling, rappeling, glissading, belaying, placement of anchors, map reading, survival, campcraft—are not hard to master and you can be sure the instructor will proceed safely and carefully. Men and women of all ages take these courses, but you must be in good physical and mental condition. Most schools provide all equipment but not personal items like boots and gloves. Here are a few of the leading mountaineering schools in the United States.

The Bob Culp Climbing School

The Basic Rock School offers comprehensive, thorough instruction on a private or semi-private (two students only) basis. The emphasis is on safety, good sportsmanship and "clean climbing" techniques. The courses

are oriented towards the serious beginner. Reserve in advance. Fees per lesson are $26 private, $16 semi-private. There is also instruction in technical ice climbing during the cold months (same fees apply), and snow and glacier lessons in the summer ($30 semi-private, $50 private). You can contact them at 1329 Broadway, Boulder, Colorado 80302 Tel: 303-442-8355

Dick Pownall's Mountaineering School at Vail

Under the direction of Dick Pownall, Himalayan mountaineer and a member of the successful 1963 American Mt. Everest expedition, the Mountaineering

School at Vail offers all levels of instruction. The six-day basic seminar costs $195, including all meals and lodging and one night at the Kiandra Lodge in Vail. The course is limited to 10 students with 3-4 instructors. There is also an advanced course for those wishing to develop leadership ability in rock climbing.

Pownall also runs the Vail Wilderness Backpacking trips which take groups of 10 (from age 12) into the wilderness areas of the Gore Range, Mt. of the Holy Cross and New York Peaks. Six days costs $155 with meals and lodging; family discounts are available.

Write them at P.O. Box 931, Vail, Colorado 81657 Tel: 303-496-5418

Eastern Mountain Sports Climbing School

Eastern Mountain Sports is interested "in teaching people to become more competent in the mountains, particularly on longer routes in technical terrain." This is not a guide service. It emphasises the two-man rope and strives for a very low student-instructor ratio. The price per day is $20-25 for groups and $36 for individual instruction. They also point out that the White Mountains offer some of the best ice climbing in the country. Contact them at Main Street, North Conway, N. H. 03860 Tel: 603-356-5433.

Exum Mountain Guide Service and School of American Mountaineering

Glenn Exum's school has been in business for over forty years. Their guiding and instructing is all done in Grand Teton National Park (see "Family Outings"). Climbers must qualify through the school before

scheduling climbs. Exum says those in good shape usually qualify to climb the Grand Teton (a two-day climb) with one day of basic and one of intermediate instruction.

The Basic School fee is $11 per day and climbs cost about $20 per day. Write them at Grand Teton National Park, Moose, Wyoming 83012 Tel: 307-733-2297

Johann Northwest Mountain Guides

Ed Johann, a mountaineer of vast experience in the Northwest, Canada and Mexico, offers seminars on rock, ice and snow climbing. He also runs backpacking outings to mountain lakes, summit climbs to any of the major Northwest peaks and glacier travel, if you wish. He takes groups to Mexico for hiking, camping and climbing every February. The cost per day averages $20, including food. Contact them at P.O. Box 19171, Portland, Oregon 97219

A renaissance in canoeing is taking place as more and more Americans rediscover the advantages of these unique watercraft. Americans are now estimated to own over two million canoes. They find it a manageable kind of challenge to human skill and strength as well as an attractive form of recreation. The canoe is quiet, easily portaged, non-polluting, swift and unobtrusive in addition to being moderately priced. It appeals to many who like to slip gently along a quiet lakeside at dusk, watching for deer and waterfowl, and at the same time to those who welcome the thrill of battling their way down rapids and through whitewaters and value the maneuverability of the canoe under such conditions.

We have selected three outfits which offer you a chance to enjoy this traditional outdoors activity, together with some information on kayaking and rafting. They, too, are growing water sports.

AMERICAN RIVER TOURING ASSOCIATION, CALIFORNIA

"To flow with the river is to plug-in to the powers of nature without wasting them," says Lou Elliot, Director of the American River Touring Association (ARTA). "You go with the current, and feeling the river's energy puts you in touch with your own energy source." A river trip is a great way to escape the problems of mechanized life. The oars dip silently into the water, and your raft follows the current to the heartlands of nature. Gone is the noise, pollution and worries of the motor-driven world; here there is peace and renewed faith in the beauty of living.

Canoeing

The canoe has been part of the American water scene since its early beginnings. Long before the European explorers arrived on the scene, the North American Indian had developed the bark canoe to a high level of design and manufacture, so much so that the present-day canoe, while more likely made of aluminum, fiberglass, formed plastics, canvas-over-wood and even cedar strip, is little changed from the original Indian design.

The explorers were impressed by the speed, light weight and load-carrying capacity of the canoe, and readily adopted it to their own use as they made their way from tidewater to the remote interior, paddling across the waterways that laced the new continent. Today's canoeists travel these same rivers—the Hudson, James, St. Lawrence, Ohio, Mississippi, Colorado, Sacramento, Columbia and Snake, among hundreds of others.

On canyon river-running trips, you often beach along the way to explore beautiful side-canyons on foot. Swimming, fishing, photography and plain relaxation add to the river experience. Comfortable camps are set up on shore, and fresh campfire meals are served up by the boatmen.

The ARTA, a non-profit organization with headquarters in Oakland, California, operates raft trips on a dozen or more different rivers in the United States and in British Columbia, South America and the Caribbean.

The outings are designed for people of all ages who love the outdoors life. Professional guides do the rowing; on some trips, canoes and kayaks are available for side trips. The ARTA operates a school for whitewater boatmen, primarily to provide guides for its own trips, but also to train people who wish to learn the skills of river running.

Costs

Trips scheduled for the public range from one to twelve days and start almost every week in the spring and summer. Prices range from $40 for a one-day trip on a California river to $550 for a 16-day oar-power Grand Canyon river and trail expedition that combines river running the Colorado through the Grand Canyon with hikes into remote reaches of Silver Grotto, Matkatamiba, Nautilod and other beautiful and relatively unexplored side canyons. Costs are all-inclusive; you furnish your own basic back-packing equipment, or it can be rented from ARTA for about $20 per person.

Their American White-Water School classes range from two days for $28 to their professional river guide course of 33 days for $600. For more information contact the American River Touring Association at 1016 Jackson Street, Oakland, California 94607, Telephone 415-465-9355.

NANTAHALA OUTDOOR CENTER, NORTH CAROLINA

While the last Olympics introduced canoeing events to a national audience, it was the film *Deliverance* that vividly depicted the thrill and challenge of the whitewater experience. If the movie whetted your interest in running rapids, you can take a rafting expedition offered by the Nantahala Outdoor Center down the Chattooga River on which the picture was made. Your guide might even be Payson Kennedy, who served as river guide and canoeing double in the film production. However, river rafting expeditions are really only one aspect of activities at the Center, which is seriously concerned with instruction in the use of open and decked canoes, kayaks and rafts

for running whitewaters.

The area in which the Center is located in western North Carolina just south of Great Smoky Mountain National Park, is known for its swift rivers and white waters. The "Week of Rivers" whitewater clinics offered by the Center takes advantage of the variety of rapids-running opportunities and programs six days of instruction on progressively more difficult rivers.

Whitewater training clinics are held year round and are conducted by John Payson Kennedy, thirty-year canoeing professional, assisted by a staff which includes paddlers from the 1972 U.S. Olympic Team and the 1973 World Championship U.S. team. Classes meet the needs of paddlers of all types of boats and levels of skill from beginner to advanced. Individual instruction can be arranged.

You may bring your own white water equipment and boat, or rent them at the Center. You will need spray skirt, helmet, life jacket, wet suit during colder months, and plenty of warm clothes at any time of the year. Camping equipment is required for the Week of Rivers clinics during which the group camps out each evening. Since the

Champion canoeist on the Nantahala

Center has a limited supply of camping equipment for rental, check beforehand or plan to bring your own.

Costs

Clinics in kayak, decked canoe and open canoe range from $50 for two days to five and six-day Week of Rivers for $125 and $150. Fee includes instruction, text materials, and meals. Equipment, including boat, will cost from $15 for the two-day kayak class to $50 for the six-day decked boat class. Accommodations are available at the Center motel at moderate rates.

Rafting expeditions in a 12-foot heavy-duty river raft down eight miles of the Nantahala River, which culminate with a breath-taking run through Nantahala Falls, cost $10 per person. A rafting trip down the Chattooga through some spectacular rapids, costs $20 per person. The cost includes rafts, life preservers, paddles and bailers; trained, experienced whitewater guides accompany each group of rafters. The most dangerous rapids are scouted in advance and instructions on the best techniques for running each rapid is given. Paddlers are encouraged to walk around any rapids they feel may be more dangerous than fun. Rafters must be in good health and unafraid of water. Children under seven are not allowed on the Nantahala trip and must be at least 13 on the Chattooga trip. Baby-sitting for younger children can be arranged. The Center will also provide guides and arrange trips to suit individual requirements and interests.

Camping in the Quetico-Superior Wilderness

Other attractions include hiking (the Appalachian Trail crosses the Nantahala River nearby the Center), rock-climbing, rock-hounding, foraging trips and nature walks. There is also horseback riding: you may take a guided lunch or dinner ride, or an overnighter to local points of interest.

To start learning, or to improve your whitewater technique, contact:
*Nantahala Outdoor Center,
Star Route Box 68, Bryson City,
North Carolina 28713
Tel. 704-488-6407*

WILDERNESS OUTFITTERS, MINNESOTA

The Quetico-Superior canoe country, lying on both sides of the Minnesota-Ontario border, encompasses some twelve-thousand square miles of uninhabited wilderness which beckons to be explored. In this land of inter-connected lakes and pine-clad forest, the canoe is the ideal means of travel. Wilderness Outfitters, in Ely, Minnesota, which claims to be the world's oldest canoe outfitting firm (dating back to 1921), is organized to provide everything required to explore the area by water. Just bring your personal clothing and fishing tackle; if necessary, the outfitter can provide these too.

Their basic canoe trip has a practically unlimited selection of destinations from which to choose, both on the American side in Superior National Forest, and on the Canadian side in Quetico Provincial Park. Border-crossing procedures are uncomplicated. The outfitter will "launch" you at various starting points, providing you with canoe, paddles, tent, all camping and cooking equipment, food, full instructions including a map, even an outboard motor, and a guide if you'd like, although the outfitter insists guides are not necessary. Once launched, you're on your own. You can paddle through woodland lakes, down little rivers, portage from lake to lake, pitch your tent and camp along the lakeside. You can go fishing, hiking, exploring, bird and animal watching, or simply allow civilization to slide away and nature to take over. Wilderness Outfitters can also provide airborne transportation to remote lakes (the plane carries the canoe, too) from which you paddle back to a starting point. As you fly over the route, you can mark on your map promising places to camp, fish, and explore on your return trip.

For those who want to settle down in one place immediately, the outfitter will take you by motor boat to secluded tent cabins on Basswood Lake. Each camp site is well-separated from the others, and comes completely equipped with camping and cooking gear, food, an aluminum boat and outboard motor (canoes can be rented). There are also boat fishing trips on Basswood Lake with tent accommodations, at a budget price.

For the ardent fisherman, there's a Fly-In to Lac de Mille Lacs Lake on the Canadian side, which is the fastest reproducing walleye lake in the Province of Ontario. The largest walleye caught so far by a guest was 12½-pounds and the largest northern pike was 25¼-pounds. There are two cabins here that accommodate four

people each, and one cabin that houses six people. The entire camp can be reserved for your party.

Rates

Canoe trips are $14 per person per day; tent cabin trips cost $149.50 per person for a minimum of five days; boat fishing trips are $99 per person for five days, and "Fly-In Canadian Outpost Cabins" (a five-day trip for a party of two or more) is $175 per person. Children under 16 go at half-rate when in a party of two adults, except for the Fly-In trips. You'll need fishing licenses; and, if you go across the border into Quetico Park, there are

taxes on canoes ($2 per day) and on food (40c per day after the second day).

Ely can be reached by good highways from Minneapolis-St. Paul and from Duluth, where there is also daily bus service. There's an all-weather airport at Ely, and if you fly in the outfitter will provide free ground transportation while you are there.

For additional details and reservations, which should be made well in advance, contact

Wilderness Outfitters, Inc., 1 East Camp Street, Ely, Minnesota 55731. Tel. 218-365-3211.

Family Outings

Family outings no longer have to be the stereotyped vacation at the seashore, a week at a cabin on a lake, or even motel-hopping along America's highways. There are a growing number of alternatives and we invite your attention to four changes of scenery that may interest you.

Grand Teton, Wyoming

Grand Teton National Park sprawls over 33,000 acres in northwestern Wyoming, encompassing some of the most majestic and breathtaking scenery found anywhere in the world. Deeded to the Federal government in 1949 by John D. Rockefeller, Jr., the preserve teems with protected animal species including bison and the rare trumpeter swan.

There are nineteen mountains in the Teton Range that tower above 10,000 feet. The Grand Tetons are a kaleidoscope of color from the deep purples and colder blues to the warm reds of dancing sunlight. Local people say that the mountains never look the same from one minute to the next.

Jackson Lake is the largest (but certainly not the only) spring-fed lake in the Park, and the Snake River is the major waterway through the area.

The family can enjoy everything from hiking and fishing to water sports, golf, and tennis. Nearby facilities include rafting down the Snake River and day trips to Yellowstone.

Accommodations are as varied as

Scenic float trip down the Snake River in Grand Teton National Park

the activities. The Grand Teton Lodge Company manages three extensive complexes starting with Jackson Lake Lodge where the cost of rooms ranges from $25 to $45 per person per day (no charge for children under 12).

The rustic and isolated Jenny Lake Lodge has private cabins for its guests and the rates are $70 per day for two with breakfast and dinner. Four people sharing a two-bedroom cabin would be billed $135 including two meals.

At Colter Bay Village, a log cabin with two rooms and connecting bath runs about $30 per day per person. Meals are not included. There are also tent cabins with kitchen facilities at a cost of $9 per per person for groups of four.

The Grand Teton Lodge Company prefers that you arrive by public transportation and use the park's bus system to get around. Bicycling is also very popular and bikes can be rented at the Park. There are also grounds for campers and motorhomes.

For more information, contact the Grand Teton Lodge Company, Moran, Wyoming 83013.

Camping In Europe

If you have been searching for an unusual and economical way of seeing Europe that allows you to move at your own pace, consider the rental of a fully outfitted VW camper. It's no problem to bed down in the Bois de Boulogne right in the center of Paris, pitch a tent in the Tuscan Hills above Florence, or camp among the elves deep in the Black Forest. Even in July and August when the Continent is a haven for tourists, you can obtain space easily at almost any campground.

Convenience, a casual approach, and modest cost are only a few of the benefits of camping. It is also a guaranteed way to get off the tourist circuit and mingle with vacationing Europeans from many countries. The camaraderie of camping life makes introductions as basic as sharing a glass of wine, and there will always be children from other lands for your youngsters to play with.

Continental Campers, Inc. offers a selection of VW buses completely outfitted for camping. All vehicles come with auxiliary tents, bedding, stove, refrigerator, sink, pots, pans, dishes, cups, glasses, and utensils. The VW Campmobile can comfortably sleep five, while a Microbus can accommodate larger families. Campers are picked up and returned to Amsterdam.

Rentals are based on the week and the fees depend on the time of year plus how far you plan to drive. As an example, a VW Campmobile with unlimited mileage in late spring or early fall rents for about $225 per week. In the summer, the same vehicle would be $260. During April and May, you can rent the Campmobile for a month at about $500.

Campsite charges, even at the more luxurious complexes with swimming pools, are less than the cost of a room at a third class hotel. Food expenses decrease proportionately with the amount of cooking you do yourself. In fact, the only significant cost you will incur beyond the vehicle rental is for gasoline which tends to be about twice as high as it is in the United States.

Additional information and reservations are available from Continental Campers, Inc., 84 State Street, Boston, Massachusetts 02109. Telephone: 617-523-0460. Ask about their combination airfare-camper packages.

Nature With A Naturalist

Garrett De Bell, a young naturalist with credentials in teaching (University of California, Berkeley) and editing (*The Environmental Handbook*), conducts special tours stressing the flora and fauna of three still pristine areas: the Baja, Sierra Nevada, and the Hawaiian Islands of Kauai, Maui, and Hawaii.

In keeping with the philosophy of observing nature without disturbing it, De Bell limits the size of his groups. As an example, his one-week High Sierra Trek with backpacks is limited to a maximum enrollment of 15. Itineraries tend to be fluid and layover points in all three areas are governed by current conditions.

The Baja trips concentrate on the littoral life along the Pacific shoreline and on observing the gray whale which frequents the area. Much of this tour is conducted by boat. If you select the High Sierra Trek, emphasis is placed on animal life indigenous to those mountains. Backpacking and survival techniques are taught as an adjunct to the trip.

The many faces of the Hawaiian

Setting up for the night in a Campmobile

Cutting through a snowy field in Woodstock

Islands are highlighted in the tour of this island group. Shore life is studied on Kauai; rain forests on Maui; and the volcano Mauna Loa on Hawaii.

The cost of these expeditions vary considerably. A three-day Sierra hike would cost about $60, while the Hawaiian excursion would be more than $700 including round-trip airfare from San Francisco. Garrett De Bell also designs and operates custom trips in these and other areas. Full particulars are available by writing to Garrett De Bell Natural History

Trips, Suite 154, 770 Welch Road. Palo Alto, California 94304.

Ski Touring, Vermont

More than 1,000 years ago, the mountain people of Norway discovered that the best way to get around and enjoy the countryside in the middle of winter was on a pair of walking skis secured only at the front of each foot. With an easily learned slide-and-glide motion and a pair of long poles, they could traverse all but the most snow-drifted terrain. Today, ski touring, as it is called, is a growing and invigorating winter pastime.

Its joys are several. View it as the winter equivalent of hiking over well-marked, but hardly used trails. The privacy is a treasure, because most skiers are busy with the slopes and overlook this vigorous form of exercise. Ski touring is readily accessible almost anywhere there is snow; it is quickly mastered; and queuing for chair lifts isn't part of the sport.

The Woodstock Inn, in southern Vermont, maintains some 40 miles of trails which you can explore for a modest fee. Nearby, the 10-mile-long Sky Line Trail connects Woodstock with the village of Barnard. You can rent cross country skis at the Woodstock Inn.

If you enjoy the excitement of downhill skiing, the slopes of Mount Tom, Suicide Six, Killington, Ascutney, and Sugarbush are all within an hour of the town. Other pleasures in this historic section of New England include antique hunting in a myriad of crossroad towns and villages, a visit to Dartmouth College, and a chance to see the birthplace of Calvin Coolidge where his son still runs a cheese factory.

Accommodations run the gamut from the picturesque Woodstock Inn on the Village Green to motels and boarding houses. Downhill skiers use the same accommodations, so it pays to make reservations well in advance.

For reservations, contact the Woodstock Inn, Woodstock, Vermont 05091.

Start Them Young

Young people today welcome the challenge of outdoor experiences where they can build confidence in themselves and acquire skills that will provide a lifetime of enjoyment and appreciation for the outdoor world. There are a number of outstanding summer activities tailored to the needs of young people. You may be interested in any of the four we have selected.

Climbing near the Chase Ranch

The Chase Ranch, Montana

In a unique approach to the needs of young people, the Chase family offers a handful of teenagers the opportunity to glean an appreciation for the American West by sharing in its history, Indian culture, and conservation. Located on the banks of Montana's Smith River where trout fishing is a way of life, the Chase's 2,400-acre spread is a viable laboratory in one of this nation's most beautiful wilderness settings.

In addition to being an expert fly fisherman and an active conservationist with over 30 years of wilderness experience, Dr. Alston Chase is Chairman of the Philosophy Department at Macalester College. His wife Diana is equally active. She breaks and trains her own horses and spends her winters teaching in a wilderness survival school in St. Paul. Among their colleagues who frequent the Chase Ranch are fly fisherman David Engerbretson and John Bailey as well as mountaineer Kirk Waggoner, who spends his spare time as Deputy Sheriff of Cody, Wyoming.

Young people at the Chase Ranch receive expert instruction in a variety of activities. Teaching is done on practically a one-to-one basis in fly fishing, horseback riding, mountain climbing, and there is also a strong emphasis on backpacking. Falconry, swimming, marksmanship and ranch work such as riding the fence or checking on cattle are part of the summer's activities. There are also anthropological and historical field trips coupled with hiking and camping into the mountains and rangelands bordering the ranch.

For the 1975 season, the Chase Ranch will accept twenty-five young people from 13 to 18 years of age. Each guest may stay for four weeks or eight weeks. The cost is $700 per four-week session plus transportation. Dr. Alston Chase would be delighted to supply additional information if you contact him at:

Trout fishing in Montana

Star Island Nautical Camp, Montauk, New York

Back in 1837, Richard Henry Dana spent two years before the mast as his indoctrination to the sea. Few boys today have that opportunity, yet the sea still holds that mystical fascination for youngsters everywhere. Star Island Nautical Camp offers teenage boys the modern-day equivalent of shipping out.

Located near the superb fishing waters off Montauk Point, the camp features a full range of instruction in maritime skills. The impressive facilities include a marine science building with holding tanks for marine specimens, labs, radio workshops, a navigation room, boatbuilding shop, and a fishing tackle room. At the marina, there are slips for over 30 boats.

Star Island is a place to learn about the sea and the boys elect the program they will follow. Fishing, for example, includes instruction in bottom fishing, surf casting, boat fishing, and even trips aboard commercial boats. Boating is taught on a variety of power and sailing craft. There is also seamanship, marine science, oceanography, navigation, astronomy, radio and electronic aids, engine maintenance, boat building, maritime crafts, canoeing, scuba diving, and marlinspike seamanship.

Boys between the ages of 9 and 17 are accepted at Star Island and the camp may be opened to girls in the near future. Tuition for the eight week session is $1550. A half session costs $925. You can find out more about Star Island Nautical Camp by writing:

(Winter)

1171 Summit Avenue
St. Paul, Minnesota 55105
Telephone: 612-644-6126

(Summer)

The Chase Ranch
Millegan Route
Great Falls, Montana 59401

Star Island Nautical Camp
Star Island Road
Montauk, New York 11954
Telephone: 516-668-5050

or

P.O. Box 315
Woodbury, New York 11797
Telephone: 516-921-8686
(Winter)

Outward Bound, USA

Basically a wilderness survival school, Outward Bound operates on the tenet that young people need the chance to test themselves against the outdoor world. As each obstacle is surmounted, the participant gains confidence and self-reliance, returning to urban or suburban life with a new-found inner strength.

The course begins with an introduction to a wilderness setting and is quickly compounded with an increasingly difficult series of physical and mental challenges. Students learn to rely on themselves and their companions in situations that demand everything they've got. As skills expand, confidence grows. Activities might include mountain climbing, rafting or canoeing rivers, ski-touring, snowshoeing, sailing, and others, but each is carefully tailored to push the participant to greater and greater achievements. Outward Bound's motto is "to serve, to strive, and not to yield."

The first week focuses on physical fitness training enriched with extensive instruction in such wilderness skills as safety, search and rescue, map and compass, expedition planning, and care of the environment. Once these basics are mastered, they are tested in the field through a series of growth experiences titled an Expedition, Solo Experience, Marathon, and Final Expedition. The Solo Experience at Hurricane Island School, for example, involves spending three days alone on a small, uninhabited island.

Outward Bound programs are open to anyone over 16½ years old, and a junior program for 14 to 16 year olds will begin in 1975. There are 27 separate schools on five continents and tuition for the four-week Standard Course is $450 to $500. Outward Bound, by the way, is a non-profit organization. If you would like to learn more about their programs, contact:

Outward Bound, Inc.
165 W. Putnam Avenue
Greenwich, Connecticut 06830
Telephone: 203-661-0797

Map & Compass work at Outward Bound

Don Kerbis Tennis Ranch, Michigan

Tennis is a game that can be played and enjoyed by every member of the family. No one is too young and no family member is too old to participate. The time to learn to play tennis is in the early years and it is much easier to learn from professionals in the beginning than to correct bad habits later.

Don Kerbis has assembled a staff of twenty top tennis professionals, many of them national champions and Davis Cup Players, to teach youngsters to play the game correctly. Although Kerbis offers a full range of summer camp activities on his 120-acre ranch near Watervliet, Michigan, the emphasis is decidedly on tennis. Participants rise early, engage in calisthenics, snack on high-energy tea and honey toast, and spend a good part of their time on the courts. Closed-circuit television and stop-action cameras are used constantly to check a serve or a forehand and to help the student correct mistakes right on the spot. The teacher-student ratio is about one to four.

The standard training session for youngsters from 10 to 18 at the Don Kerbis Tennis Ranch is three–weeks long and the cost is $550. At the end of the summer, there is a one-week session for adults (cost $200) and parents can participate with their youngsters if they desire. There is also an adult session over Labor Day Weekend at a cost of $125. You can learn more about the Kerbis approach to tennis by writing to:

Don Kerbis Tennis Ranch
R.R. 1, 40-20
Watervliet, Michigan 49098
Telephone: 616-463-3151

NOTATIONS

COURTS & COURSES

Tennis
The Wickenburg Inn Tennis and Guest Ranch
Sundance, Vermont
Sea Pines Plantation
John Gardner's Tennis Ranch
Princess & Pierre Marquess, Acapulco

Golf
Sotogrande, Spain
Dar Es Salaam, Morocco
Scottish Courses and the Open
Cajuiles, Dominican Republic

Skiing
Snowbird
Bretton Woods
Les Menuires & Val Thorens

Sailing
Fully-found yachts
Windjammers
Bareboat charters
Sailing schools

Tennis

The unprecedented growth of tennis in recent years has prompted a number of leading resort complexes to modify their thinking and their physical facilities to cater to participants in this sport. There are also a number of resorts built expressly for the purpose of teaching and encouraging the playing of tennis.

Although brochures are carefully worded to show subtle differences, any serious tennis resort offers expert instruction, ball return machines, videotape machines to help the student correct faults, plenty of well-kept courts, and fellow guests who share your interests in the game. If you merely enjoy playing tennis or learning more about the game, any of the reputable resorts will satisfy your

demands. The quality player, however, who seeks opponents of equal or better skill has a more difficult search. It simply adds up to a hit-or-miss proposition, since top ranking players are not always attracted to the major resorts.

We have assembled information on several deluxe resorts around the country where tennis is a way of life.

The Wickenburg Inn Tennis and Guest Ranch

Tennis is featured at Wickenburg Inn, but this Spanish-style vacation resort ranch offers its guests much more. Located on 4,700 acres in a wind-protected valley some 60 miles from Phoenix,

Wickenburg has 11 plexipave tennis courts and a full range of of instructional equipment. Court time is unlimited, providing, of course, there are courts available. Regularly scheduled tennis clinics are part of the fare and both individual and group instruction are offered daily.

Wickenburg caters to the family. While parents play tennis, the ranch provides supervised activities for youngsters. There are corrals, a swimming pool, a rodeo arena, and even a naturalist on duty for nature walks. If you want to fish or water ski, Lake Pleasant is a half-hour away by car.

Accommodations for single, double, or family occupancy in separate Casitas or at the Ranch Lodge begin at $30 per day per person. The rate includes meals, tennis, riding, and the use of an electric cart for transportation.

Indoor courts at Sundance

You can contact your travel agent for information or reservations or you can write to the Wickenburg Inn Tennis and Guest Ranch, Wickenburg, Arizona 85358. Telephone: 602-684-7811.

Sundance

Set in the rolling hills of Vermont, Sundance prides itself on the thoroughness of its tennis workshops. In winter, there is also an opportunity to alternate between the indoor courts and the ski slopes of nearby Killington and Pico Peak.

The facilities include eight lighted clay courts and four indoor courts. The five-day intensive tennis program costs $300 per person including food and lodging. A weekend workshop averages about $135 per person. You can also enjoy swimming and sailing in the summer, plus hiking and riding on Sundance's 23 acres.

Further information is available from Sundance, 40 Curtis Avenue, Rutland, Vermont 05701. Telephone: 802-775-1971.

Sea Pines Plantation

Sea Pines, a 5,200-acre enclave on the southern tip of picturesque Hilton Head Island, is a lush resort that caters to experienced tennis players. Scattered among the three sites within Sea Pines are 30 composition courts, 7 hard courts, and 8 platform tennis courts. Instructional programs are available, but the emphasis here is on good tennis.

There are a variety of package deals available. One example is a summer four-day, three-night package that provides room and tennis for $150 per couple, but excludes meals. You are entitled to six hours of guaranteed court time as part of the deal and can play longer if courts are empty (which is not very likely in July and August). Extra time can be booked at $4 per hour on the hard courts and $8 per hour for doubles on the composite courts.

Besides tennis, Hilton Head offers a wide range of other recreational activities that includes golf on any of three courses, swimming in four pools, or excellent salt water fishing.

You can get all the literature you need by contacting Sea Pines Plantation, Hilton Head Island, South Carolina 29928. Telephone: 803-785-3322.

John Gardner's Tennis Ranch At Camelback

The game of tennis is taken seriously at John Gardner's Tennis Ranch at Camelback. It is one of the finest and most elegant tennis resorts in the country. Special tennis clinics are held for groups (beginner, intermediate and advanced) throughout the year. Camelback presently has 21 courts and is large enough to provide for instruction as well as individual play. It's a resort where the main language spoken is tennis.

Individual accommodations that include breakfast, lunch, and court time begin at $90 per day for two. Seven-day, six-night clinics, offering meals, lodging, and 22 hours of instruction plus additional court time start at $600 per person, double occupancy.

Naturally, there are swimming

Videotaping at Camelback

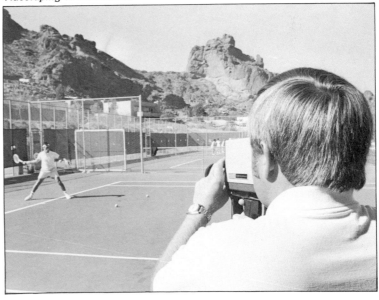

pools and sundecks at Camelback and you can ride or play golf nearby. A letter or phone call to John Gardner's Tennis Ranch at Camelback, 5700 E. McDonald Drive, Scottsdale, Arizona 85253 (telephone: 602-948-2100) will bring full particulars.

Princess and Pierre Marquess, Acapulco

If you're planning an Acapulco vacation and would like to play tennis while you are there, you may want to consider the two-hotel complex of the Princess and the Pierre Marquess. A stay at either hotel entitles you to two hours per day court time on any of the eight outdoor tennis courts and, depending on your length of stay, at least an hour on the indoor courts.

Recognize, of course, that days are warm and it can often be uncomfortably hot on the outdoor courts. If you choose to play on the outdoor courts in the evening, there is a charge of $7 per hour. An additional charge of $12 per hour is made for the indoor courts which are air conditioned.

The two hotels offer many packages. A typical three-day, two-night arrangement from December through April costs $105 per day per person double occupancy on Modified American Plan.

Bookings can be made through your travel agent.

Golf

For a non-nonsense week of 36 holes a day on world-caliber courses, few layouts can match such American complexes as Pebble Beach and Pinehurst. But if you're looking for something a little different—courses made exotic by their locations, courses steeped in golfing history—then you should look overseas. You can still squeeze in 36 holes a day, though you may well be too distracted by your environment to bother with that afternoon round.

Sotogrande, Spain

On almost half of the holes of the original 18, you can see Gibraltar looming steadfastly in the distance. For Sotogrande, a 4,000-acre resort and development, lies on the Costa del Sol between the Rock and Marbella. Its courses—two full

18-holers and a 9-holer—were all designed by Robert Trent Jones, and sport his distinctive signature. The tees are enormously long; a 5-par that plays driver/four-wood/wedge from the front markers can require a three-iron approach off the blues. The fairways are wide and deceptively forgiving; an errant drive might be in the fairway, but with no angle to the green. And the greens are breathtakingly big; the trick lies not in hitting them, but in getting close enough for two putts. Course maintenance is superb, thanks to one of the first underground sprinkling systems to be installed in Europe.

Accommodations

Accommodations are at the Sotogrande Club de Golf. They

Sotogrande

include single or double rooms and suites and range from $39 per day European Plan (without meals) to $67 per day Full American Plan (all meals), per person double occupancy in a deluxe suite.

Other pleasures at Sotogrande include a mile-long private beach on the Mediterranean, riding, polo, tennis and skeet shooting. Nearby are such southern Spanish cities as Seville and Cordoba, and a short plane hop across the Mediterranean lands you in Morocco.

For more information on Sotogrande consult your travel agent or contact:

Director of Hotels
Apartado 1
Club de Golf
Sotogrande, Cadiz
Spain

Royal Golf Club of Dar Es Salaam, Morocco

Thick stands of cork-oak trees divide the fairways of this, Morocco's premier golf complex. The 45-hole resort has been carved out of the Temara forest on the southeast perimeter of Rabat, the capital city. Golf is surprisingly popular in this North African country. This is due mainly to King Hassan II, an ardent player who numbers Billy Casper among his golfing partners. Since His Majesty's ascension to the throne, three new complexes have been built from scratch and two others have been reconditioned.

The most challenging 18 holes on Dar Es Salaam is the Red Course. Architect Robert Trent Jones made imaginative use of water on this

Dar Es Salaam

island layout, especially on the 9th hole, a 3-par where the green is perched on an island in a lake, and on the 12th, a 5-par that seems a carbon copy of Pebble Beach's famed finishing hole. The 12th hole is a double-dogleg left bordered on the left not by the Pacific Ocean but by the calm but equally penalizing waters of a lake.

Green fees at Dar Es Salaam are 30 Dirhans per day.

Accommodations ranging from modest to luxurious are available in the center of Rabat, about ten minutes away by car. Other pleasures include the nearby Royal Equestrian Club and the diverse city of Rabat itself, which lies on the Atlantic Coast.

For more information please consult your travel agent or contact *Moroccan National Tourist Office* *597 Fifth Avenue* *New York, N.Y. 10017*

The Open Courses, Scotland

The Open rotates among a handful of historic courses throughout Great Britain. Four of them—St. Andrews, Carnoustie, Troon and Prestwick—are in Scotland, the birthplace of the game, along with about 296 other layouts.

These courses welcome visiting golfers, in marked contrast to the Winged Foots, Merions and Oakmonts that are the sites of the U.S. Open. In fact, two, St. Andrews and Carnoustie, are public. There are no two and three hour waits for starting time, no crowded fairways—just the most scintillating golf you've ever played anywhere.

These courses are authentic and magnificent. They are all links, which means they have been carved out of erstwhile pastureland. Their bunkers tend to be naturally placed rather than specifically designed, and the rough is indeed a rough mixture of heather and gorse.

Green fees range from $2 at Carnoustie ($9.20 per week) to a high of $8 at Troon, a private club. A small price, indeed, to pay for playing on turf that is living history.

Probably the best way to golf the great courses of Scotland is to arrange a car hire, land at Prestwick and begin driving. Traveling "off itinerary" will give you a chance to stay at a course you especially like, dawdle in a backroads village and discover such other classic courses as Turnberry and Dalmahoy and Machrihanish. For complete travel information—maps, listings of accommodations, restaurants and courses—write the

Scottish Travel Board
23 Ravelston Terrace
Edinburgh, EH4 3EU
Scotland

or

British Travel Authority
680 Fifth Avenue
New York, N.Y. 10017

Golf Ensemble, Scotland

Scotland's munificence of fine courses makes it a prime goal for golf travel packagers. If you prefer to travel with a group to take advantage of slightly lower rates and the convenience of having most details attended to, and if the caliber of the courses played is important, look into the Scottish tours.

A typical two-week package breaks down this way: five nights at a hotel in Perthshire, with two meals a day and green fees at courses like King's and Queens' at Gleneagles, St. Andrews and Carnoustie; five nights in Turnberry to play the Ailsa and Arran courses, with optional trips to nearby Troon and Prestwick, three nights in Edinburgh to play such courses as Dalmahoy East and West. Price tag for the tour: about $1,500. For further information, contact your travel agent or

Arnold Langer
Golf International
250 W. 57th Street
New York, N.Y.

Cajuiles, Dominican Republic

There are few top-flight golf courses in the Caribbean. Of these, fewer still are not mere diversions for the casino crowd. Cajuiles is a genuine exception.

Part of a two-hotel resort development on the southern coast of the Dominican Republic, it sprawls along a rocky coast. Indeed, water is a factor of play on a third of the holes. The fairways and greens are of Bermuda grass, which calls for sweeping, rather than divot-gouging, iron shots and firm putts. Accuracy off the tees is called for; architect Peter Dye, who co-designed the Hilton Head Course with Jack Nicklaus, has studded Cajuiles with native foliage. Errant shots must be played over or through stands of cashew, coconut, teak and almond trees, or hacked out of sugar cane.

Accommodations at the Hotel Romana and the Casa de Campo vary considerably in price, depending on the season, the category of room and the package arrangement, if any. For example, in summer, which at La Romana stretches until mid-December, lodgings, two meals per day and green fees run about $250 per person per week, double occupancy.

Other activities here include tennis, skeet and trap shooting, riding and deep-sea fishing. For more information consult your travel agent or:

Hotel Romana
La Romana
Dominican Republic

Taking Your Golf Clubs With You

Should you contemplate a visit to the courses below, or to any of the other golfing resorts of the world, plan to take your own clubs. Rental sets at even the fanciest courses tend to be department store lines rather than professional lines. Most airlines will ship your clubs under a special arrangement that permits one set of clubs per passenger at $22.56 for up to 15 kilos (33 pounds), with an extra charge for added weight. If you're finicky about the brand of ball you play—especially "new generation" balls such as the Royal 6 or Wilson LD or Blue Max or Spalding Top Flite—take along a good supply. The availability of American balls can be a sometimes thing in an overseas pro shop. Finally, if you're partial to wooden tees, bring a bag or two; for some unfathomable reason, plastic tees seem to be the rage in Europe and Asia.

Skiing

These days the play is in the four-season recreation resort where the condominium apartment and townhouse provide the accommodations, and skiing is the promoted winter sport. We've selected two new year-round recreation resorts in the U.S., one in the West, the other in New Hampshire, and two in the great snow country of France, one of which you'll stay in and both of which you'll ski.

Snowbird, Utah

It averages 450 inches of snow a year, assuring dependable ski conditions from mid-November through April. It's in the Wasatch National Forest, just half-an-hour from Salt Lake city, with easy access by plane, train, and highway. It's *Snowbird,* a resort in the new condominium tradition, where skiing is the big idea.

Snowbird has the terrain and the facilities to match all that snow. Wide powder bowls and swiftly sloping meadows build confidence in the beginner and intermediate skier, while machine-packed runs offer challenge to the expert. The *Snowbird* aerial tramway carries 1,000 skiers per hour to the top of 11,000-foot Hidden Peak. From there on down there's something to please almost everyone, with runs up to 2½ miles long. Both packed and powder runs are served by three high-capacity double chairlifts, and there's another double chairlift just for the first-time and novice skiers.

Accommodations

Three condominium lodges and a full-service hotel offering 591 bedrooms, studios, suites and dormitories as well as ten restaurants and snack bars, provide a complete range of lodging and meals for every taste. Facilities include ski shop, ski school, medical clinic, men's and women's saunas, ski lockers, heated swimming pools, laundry rooms, card rooms, and boutiques.

Rates

Snowbird rates are as varied as its facilities. You can choose to stay in a suite, a studio, a bedroom or a dormitory, with single to quintuple occupancy, on daily or three, five, and seven-night packages, or group rates, with or without lift tickets, and ski week options. As an example, a bedroom at the Lodge, double occupancy, is $21 per person per day, meals and lift tickets extra.

For brochures and reservations contact

Snowbird,
Snowbird, Utah 84070
Telephone: 801-742-2222

The Village At Bretton Woods

Across the country, in the heart of the White Mountains, New Hampshire is the *The Village of Bretton Woods,* a new four-season recreational community that provides accommodations in condominium townhouses and in its own motor lodge for visiting skiers who come to run its trails.

From its location at the base of Mt. Washington (6,288 feet, highest peak in the Northeast), Bretton Woods runs two new chair lifts and a T-bar to carry skiers to the top of its seven trails, with runs up to a mile long, and a 1,100-foot vertical drop. On the way down, skiers enjoy a spectacular view of the Presidential Range. Snow-making equipment helps keep key sections of the slope covered, improving the natural conditions and prolonging the season.

Cross-country skiing is an added attraction at Bretton Woods. Thirty kilometers of scenic trails wind through old railroad beds and carriage roads along the Ammonoosuc River in the valley. If you go, don't miss the Bota Tour—a five-mile cross-country trip with lunch (wine and food cooked over an open fire).

Accommodations

There are sixty rooms in the motor lodge, plus two and four bedroom townhouse, available for daily or longer rental. There's also a new, modern four-story Sports Lodge which houses among other attractions a gourmet restaurant, gameroom and sports shop.

Rates

You can choose a three-day ski package that includes room at the motor lodge, meals, lift ticket and lessons, from $80, double occupancy. A five-day package, also double occupancy, would be $134. Single occupancy for either package would be slightly higher. Juniors (under 14) are charged about 15% lower rates. Room with meals, perhaps for family or friend who does not ski: three days $54, five days $88. Townhouses can accommodate six people in two bedrooms or twelve people in four bedrooms—rates on request. For brochures and reservations contact:

The Village at Bretton Woods
Bretton Woods,
New Hampshire 03575
Telephone: 603-278-1000

Double-chairlift, Bretton Woods

Les Menuires & Val Thorens

The French have added a new symbol to skiing—*SNO*. It means that nine leading French ski resorts have banded together to provide the skier with access to an electronic reservation system which, with one telephone call, gives complete, immediate information and will make reservations free of charge at any one of the nine resorts. In addition, *SNO* cards delivered in each resort are valid for the lifts at the eight others.

In the heart of the three valleys in Savoy, close to the Swiss border, is *Les Menuires*, with its great, wide slopes and up the road, nestled against the glacier, is *Val Thorens*, an extraordinary place to ski both winter and summer.

We suggest staying in *Les Menuires*, where you can choose from an eye-arresting array of ultra-modern hotels and rentable condominium apartments and visiting *Val Thorens*, either by road or up and over one of the lifts that now connect these two resorts.

It's a multi-lingual world with just about everything required to serve the skier's needs. If you're seeking some of the very best skiing overseas, in an area that is also rich with indoor and outdoor activities *apres le ski*, this place deserves your serious consideration.

Accommodations

Les Menuires is a modern four-season vacation resort with a heavy investment in *le ski*. There are 19 ski lifts (four with cabins) which put you on top of 100 miles of ski runs and thousands of acres of wide-open, snow-covered slopes. There are 7,500 beds in the hotels, and professional services embracing supermarkets, boutiques, sports shops, and medical, physiotherapy and child daycare centers.

Rates

You can expect to pay 100 francs per person per day, single occupancy, with all meals, in a three-star hotel, slightly less in a two-star, and about 20% less in either instance with double occupancy.

Rates are affected by such variables as number of people in hotel room or apartment; number of meals taken; month of the year; holidays; even whether the windows face north or south (south can be 10% higher).

For example, a two-room apartment accommodating four people would cost about 1,700

francs for the twelve days of Christmas, to which you would add the cost of food and wine, maid service, ski lifts (25 to 35 francs per day), ski school, and the other entertainments. And while the dollar-to-franc ratio may vary, you can be certain that there will be snow—lots of it.

For information and reservations contact your travel agent or

SNO
16 Boulevard Haussman
Paris 75008 France

Taking Skis With You

Under rates agreed to by the major international airlines, one set of ski equipment (skis, poles and boots) can be included at the special baggage rate of $11 each way, from the United States. Domestic airlines will carry your skis for free. If lugging skis and poles becomes too onerous, at least take your boots. Skis and poles can be rented, but your own boots are going to fit with far more comfort than those you rent.

Sailing

Perhaps you would like to get away from land entirely, and spend your time outdoors on the water. There are all kinds of sailing holidays for you to take this year, no matter what kind of sailor you are. They range from a Learn-to-Sail course at the Palmas del Mar resort in Puerto Rico to the bareboat charter of a ketch or a yawl in the Grenadines. It all depends on your mood.

You can laze around in the sun on the deck of *Rollicker* or *Invictus* while the crew makes dinner and trims the sails, or take up the challenge of sailing the yacht-of-your-choice leisurely from island to island with only your family as crew.

And then there are windjammers, large sailing ships reminiscent of the passenger-carrying merchant marine fleet a century ago, which will take you and a few dozen other would-be sailors for a casual, foggy trip up the coast of Maine, across the Atlantic, or through the Danish archipelago.

But it's time to stop dreaming about the suntan you're going to get, pick yourself up and find a boat. Here are some beautiful sailboats to choose from, and information on a few excellent sailing schools where you can polish up your seamanship.

Invictus

FULLY-FOUND YACHTS

Cruising the Dalmatian Coast:

Grace, a 114' staysail schooner, designed by R.A. Mylne and built of teak over oak by Camper & Nicholsons, to Lloyds 100 A1 + specifications. Accomodations for up to eight in five large guest cabins, three with double berths, two with single berths, and two marble-decked heads with showers. Multi-lingual captain and five in crew are berthed forward, assuring privacy. A magnificent sailing yacht, auxiliary diesel power, full electronics and navigational equipment; 40 hp Boston Whaler for water skiing. Sports equipment includes water skiis, snorkeling gear, underwater camera, even shotgun for clay target shooting.

Rates

$4,200 per week, Greek Plan, which means you pay $12 extra per day per person for gourmet meals prepared by continental chef. Wines and liquors are extra, and so are port charges (depending on the destinations you select).

Cruising the Windward & Leeward Islands:

Rollicker, a 47' fiberglass diesel auxiliary staysail ketch sailing out of Antigua. Sleeps six in three air-conditioned double cabins, two heads with showers, spacious after-main cabin. Captain and crew of one have self-contained quarters forward. *Rollicker* is a U.S. Documented yacht and carries complete electronics and navigational equipment. Also carries snorkle and scuba gear, underwater still and movie cameras, dinghy with outboard and sail, and sportboat for snorkeling, scuba and beaching in search of shells.

Rates

Winter: from $1, 372 for two people to $1, 895 for six, per week. Summer: from $1,127 for two to $1, 553 for six, per week. Includes everything but liquor.

Cruising Japanese waters out of Tokyo:

Cynara, a 93' gaff-rigged ketch, perhaps the only traditional (non-junk) yacht available in the area. Sleeps six in three double cabins, has a huge mahogany-panelled cabin for dining and entertaining. Captain and crew are berthed forward. Meals feature both Japanese and continental cuisine.

Rates

Rates are tied to a ratio of yen to the dollar and are at present about $6,000 per week, including everything but wine and liquors.

Cruising Northeastern waters out of New York:

Invictus, a Tripp-designed Columbia 57' built in 1970. For the racing or the cruising sailor. Sleeps six in three staterooms and has two heads with showers. A crew of two is berthed forward. Has full electronic and navigational equipment and diesel auxiliary engine.

Rates

Rate is $2,200 per week with crew of two, out of New York, exclusive of wine and liquors.

Adventure

WINDJAMMERS

Denmark and the Caribbean

Sailing Danish waters in the summer, and the Caribbean during the fall, winter and spring is *Hans Christian Anderson*, a 170', 500-ton, diesel-powered, three-masted schooner, built in 1973 to Lloyds 100 A1+ specifications. Accommodations for thirty-six passengers in eighteen outside, air-conditioned cabins, decorated in Danish style with lower beds only, each with private bath. There are wide decks for strolling and sunbathing, a dance floor in the saloon plus an intimate bar and spacious dining area. Meals feature continental cuisine and include a daily *Smorgastable* loaded with Scandinavian specialties. The ship is operated by a young crew of eighteen who see to it that guests have fun. To help keep the activities moving, there are motor launches, sailing dinghies, water skiing, snorkeling and fishing gear (the fishing in Denmark is excellent), and bicycles for a spin at island tie-ups.

Rates

Six-night, seven-day voyages stopping off at Danish islands in the archipelago leave Copenhagen every Sunday afternoon from late May through the middle of September. $469 per person in double cabins, includes all meals and use of the ship's sporting equipment. A limited number of single cabins are available.

Fully-found charter of the whole boat for one week is $15,750 for 36 people. Trans-Atlantic, three-week voyage, with stops at Bermuda and Azores is $600 complete.

Six-night, seven-day voyages in the Caribbean mostly between the islands of Martinique and St. Vincent via the Grenadines. $469 per person, same as the Danish trips above.

New England and the Grenadines

Sailing offshore New England in the summer, and wintering in the Grenadines between Granada and St. Lucia is *Harvey Gamage,* a spanking new 110' gaff-rigged schooner. Two weeks in the Caribbean begins with four nights at the Holiday Inn on St. Lucia or Grenada. Then you board *Harvey Gamage* for a six-day voyage, docking each night at another island in the Grenadines. The last five nights are spent at the Holiday Inn on the other island.

The *Harvey Gamage* is also available as a fully-found charter for 24 people. One week in the summer costs $6,500, all inclusive.

Maine:

Cruising Maine waters in the summer is *Adventure,* a 120' gaff-rigged, working schooner that is certified by the U.S. Coast Guard. Her voyages offer the "seagoin' way of life." You can help sail the ship by taking the helm, or learn to navigate on the chart, help to weigh anchor or haul up sail, and give a hand to keeping all shipshape and Bristol fashion. You can also sunbathe, visit with your shipmates, go fishing and take photographs. *Adventure* has accommodations for 37 people. Mealtimes feature hearty New England cookery, with a beachside

Down East lobster cookout on each voyage. Adventure leaves Camden on the first morning tide Mondays and returns early Saturday afternoon. The weekly cruise is never set, for the course is determined by the current winds and tides. Each night is spent in quiet anchorage off the coast from Portland to Bar Harbor.

Rates

$175 per person during July and August, somewhat less in June and September. Minimum age is 16 years. Price is all inclusive.

BAREBOAT CHARTERS

You get the boat complete, except for food and fuel. Arrangements can be made to have food and fuel put aboard prior to your arrival and, under certain circumstances, you may be able to hire a complete or partial crew.

Charters

In the Virgin Islands, there are sloops, cutters, ketches and yawls available, ranging in size from 31' to 45'. In the winter the rates run from $575 to $1,100; in the summer, from $425 to $700.

In the Grenadines, there are sloops, yawls and cutters available, measuring 31' to 42'. In the winter, rates run from $560 to $900; in the summer from $350 to $650.

Information

For brochures and reservations on all of the sailing above, with the exceptions of those noted below, please contact:

*V.E.B. Nicholson & Sons
9 Chauncey Street, Suite 50
Cambridge, Massachusetts 02138
Telephone: 617-661-8174*

For Invictus:

*Sparkman & Stephens, Inc.
11 E. 44th Street
New York, N.Y. 10017
Telephone: 212-MU2-3557*

For Adventure:

*Capt. Jim Sharp
Schooner Adventure
Box 696, Camden, Maine 04843
Telephone: 207-236-4449.*

SAILING SCHOOLS

"Man overboard, sail trim, hull speed, heavy weather, navigation and spinnaker techniques"—these are just a few areas in which you may want to be proficient as a beginning or advanced sailor. The sailing schools below will teach you this and much more, in friendly classes on and off the water. Located in traditional sailing waters like Martha's Vineyard and Chesapeake Bay, or at luxurious, sunny resorts like Sea Pines Plantation, Hilton Head Island, South Carolina or the new Palmas del Mar resort on the southeastern coast of Puerto Rico, the sailing schools also offer you an excuse for a wonderful and useful vacation. So if you are tired of being the cook, learn to be the skipper, or take the whole family down and prepare for that cruise you'd like to take. Even racing skipper; or take the whole family coaching from champion sailors will find it here, courtesy of the Offshore Sailing School.

Offers instruction only, but on all levels including a wide variety of correspondence courses in advanced subjects like coastal and celestial navigation. The school is under the direction of Paul J. Miller, former Naval Academy sailing coach. Tuition ranges from $72.50 for a 12-hour basic course at Marina del Rey to $195 for a 24-hour Racing course.

Offshore Sailing School

5 E. 40th Street
New York, N.Y. 10016
Telephone: 212-689-3050

Courses are offered at City Island, New York; at the Harborside Inn, Martha's Vineyard, Cape Cod, Massachusetts; at Palmas del Mar, Puerto Rico and at Sea Pines Plantation, Hilton Head Island, South Carolina. Accommodations and reservations are available through the school.

Under the direction of Steve Colgate, expert racer and sailing instructor, and his wife Doris, Offshore offers Learn-to-Sail, Learn-to-Cruise and Learn-to-Race courses, Raceweeks and even Navigation workshops and sailing vacations for their graduates who join their Sail Away Club. Teaching boats in use are Lasers, Force Fives and 27' Olympic Solings. Family members may take different courses simultaneously at the resort-based schools, so that they may spend their free time together. Tuition ranges from $145-195 a course, whether or not it is spread out over a month, a three-day weekend, or a week's vacation. Racing workshops run higher.

Annapolis Sailing School

601 6th Street, P.O. Box 1669,
Annapolis, Md. 21404
Tel: 301-267-7205
or the Sailing Lodge at the
Sheraton Inn,
P.O. Box 14414, St. Petersburg,
Fla. 33733
Tel: 813-867-1151
Offers courses in Chesapeake Bay in June to September and in St. Petersburg, Florida all year round.

Basic or advanced sailing courses, in one weekend or four, or even a five-day intensive. Tuition is $95 for 12 hours. Well-developed cruising vacations are offered where you have your own boat and may fill it with family and friends but sail in a small fleet under the supervision of a lead boat. $270 for five days on a 24' Rainbow that sleeps two to $565 for a Newport 30' that sleeps seven.

California Sailing Academy

Marina del Rey, CA 90291
Telephone: 213-821-3433

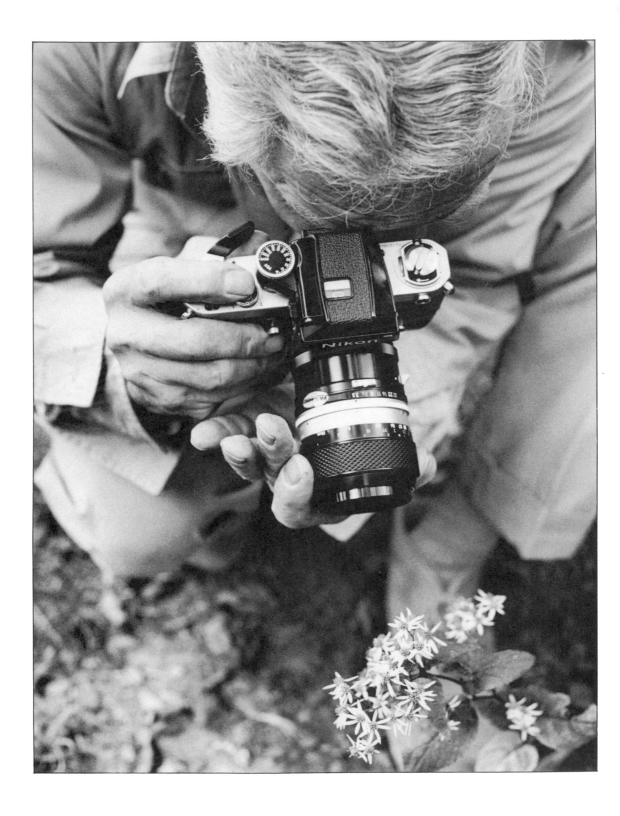

ENRICHING YOUR OUTDOOR EXPERIENCE

Outdoor Observations
Capturing Your Experience on Film
Choosing and Using Binoculars
Conservation Organizations

OUTDOOR OBSERVATIONS

It's been said that most people can't find the proverbial needle in the haystack simply because they aren't looking for a needle in a haystack. To glean the maximum from any outdoor experience, one must develop his senses and enlarge his powers of observation. This comes with practice as well as mental discipline.

If you live in a metropolitan area, you probably pay little attention to the traffic that streams by endlessly, but the screech of brakes will get your attention instantly. You will hear and recognize it over most other sounds and respond. It's not that the screech of brakes is louder than anything else, but it is a sound that your mind recognizes as a danger signal and you react.

As you walk down the street in a city or town, a sea of faces passes you in several directions. Unless you were concentrating on it, you couldn't describe the physical features of most people who passed within the last thirty seconds. Your mind has learned to accept people as part of the passing scene. It is only the unusual that will trigger a reaction. If you saw someone you knew, a recognition signal would be flashed in your brain and your friend would instantly stand out from the faceless crowd.

We are conditioned to life in urban or suburban regions. The skilled outdoorsman who can spot a fish or animal before anyone else or who hears the distant cry of a bird above the usual outdoor noises doesn't boast any powers that are different from those of his city cousin. He has merely conditioned his senses to respond to another set of stimuli.

Training our senses takes time and concentration. The secret is to accept the commonplace in nature and look for those things that don't fit into the pattern, however subtle they may be. The easiest place to begin is with movement. When you are walking in the woods, in the fields, or cruising on the water, you should respond to any type of movement you see. When something moves, it is alive and that's what you are looking for. As you become more sophisticated, you will detect slight movements. A gentle breeze may be causing the trees to sway gently and your brain automatically accepts this as it does a sea of faces on the street. Then, you notice that one limb is moving more than the others or in a direction against the breeze. This should tell you that a bird, squirrel, monkey, or other creature may be causing that branch to move and it warrants more of your attention.

The same concepts apply to sound. You learn to accept the din as part of the scene, but remain unconsciously alert to any variation.

You can even practice these techniques in the city. There is a certain amount of birds and wildlife within the city limits and you can concentrate on seeing these. Or, if you want to test the procedure, tell yourself you want to be alerted every time a red car passes. Your mind should respond.

Getting back to that needle in the haystack, the shell collector may walk a beach with millions of shells on it or a woodsman may walk by hundreds and even thousands of trees and shrubs. Suddenly, one object gains the response and the shell collector stoops to pick it up or the woodsman moves closer to admire the rare flower. Part of this stems from a basic knowledge of the subject matter and what is valuable to view or collect. Once you know that, your mind will alert you if you concentrate on what you are doing.

Spotting fish either on the surface or underwater is a learned response that has deeper roots in experience or observation rather than how sharp one's eyes may be. In clear water, you must look *through* the surface as if it were a pane of glass and concentrate on the bottom and intermediate levels. It's a scanning process in which your mind accepts all types of things but rings the bell at a specific shape or movement.

Birding

Birding can become one of the most absorbing and interesting outdoor activities. It can be an end in itself or it can be an adjunct to any other activity. The equipment is simple. All you need is a good pair of binoculars and a field guide to help you identify the species you see.

Most birders begin to keep a life list, which is nothing more than a record of the various species they have seen. A meaningful life list is one in which no species is accepted until positive identification is made. Life lists are kept in a variety of ways. Some birders merely place an "X" next to the listing in the field guide, while others will check it in the front of the guide or keep separate books and records of birds seen.

Serious birders will travel far and spend countless hours just to observe other species. Birding, however, is a great way to pass time anywhere. You can do it for a few minutes at a time while waiting for others to gather to participate in some activity.

There are a number of different field guides on the market and most of them are of excellent quality. Perhaps the most popular are "The Petersen Field Guide Series" published by Houghton Mifflin Company in Boston. Doubleday publishes a short series and Golden Press has some.

Animals

Whether your primary interest is in fishing, hunting, hiking, canoeing, or any other outdoor activity, observing wildlife in their natural habitat is an extension of the total outdoor experience. Some animals are easy to spot and you can delight in watching their antics as they pursue their normal routine. Others are more difficult to see.

Animal or game-viewing reaches the height of the art in places such as Africa where viewing safaris are well-established and the number of animals legendary. However, you can pursue this interesting facet almost anywhere, starting with squirrels and rabbits near home. There are field guides published to help you identify the animals and there are other guides that will assist you in identifying the tracks they make.

Binoculars are always helpful in game viewing, but you can frequently spot animals without the aid of optics. You will find, however, that it is far more interesting to study an animal when you use binoculars to enlarge the image.

Plants, Trees, and Flowers

Being able to identify the various species of plants, trees, and flowers can make an outing so much more meaningful. It is an easy thing to learn if you are willing to use a field guide and take the time to make some of the easier identifications. No matter where you live and where you travel, there is always something green around and you can begin to record those plants, trees, and flowers that you have seen.

Using A Field Guide

Field guides are organized to facilitate identification. The preface to the book will tell you how it can be used best and it is worth studying this before using the volume. If you are interested in the subject and are willing to do a bit of homework, you can make it a lot easier and quicker to make positive identification. Let's concentrate on the bird guides since they are by far the best sellers.

Unless you are experienced, your chances of identifying a very rare bird for a given location are minimal. The first step is to look through the book repeatedly whenever you have a spare moment. Familiarize yourself with the different groups of birds so that you can start your research in the

correct family or, at least eliminate certain families. Research and identification is just as much a process of elimination.

Your first task is to narrow the species down so that you can find the exact bird. Most of the guides use illustrations of silhouettes in addition to portraits of the birds to help you make the identification. And they emphasize the distinguishing features. Remember that size of the bird is based on field measurements of live birds and the average family member would be closer to the minimum size.

It goes without saying that a field guide is designed for use in the field and it should be carried with you whenever you are in the outdoors. If you plan to travel to a different area of the country or the world, you will probably need additional field guides. These should be purchased as far ahead of time as possible and studied to help you recognize the families. You'll find that once you get involved in bird identification, it won't take you long to select the families, even though you are halfway around the world.

Finally, spend a few minutes learning the topography of a bird so you can understand the description. When the guide refers to crown, nape, secondaries, or other features, you should know what is meant.

Field guides on other subjects are similar in design and organization. It is a matter of identifying the right family or group and understanding the features so that the descriptions in the guide are meaningful to you.

Your bookseller can obtain for you

a list of the "Peterson Field Guide Series" or write Houghton Mifflin Company, 2 Park Street, Boston, Mass. 02107.

CAPTURING YOUR EXPERIENCE ON FILM

One of the most rewarding aspects of travel is the ability to relive your trip over and over again if you are willing to invest the time and effort required to record it properly on film. It's a lot easier to show your friends what your adventures were like rather than try to tell them about it, and it is a long-term sense of satisfaction to reminisce about places you've been and things you have done.

Photography today is easy. The basic cameras are quite capable of producing good results in daylight and, if you own more sophisticated equipment, you can work miracles with just a little imagination and initiative. The difference between good pictures and great photographs is nothing more than some mental gymnastics of composition and an understanding of what the camera will record on film. Professionals seem to work quickly, quietly, and effectively, because they are familiar with their equipment, know how to use it, and concentrate on "seeing" the picture. They already know that the film will record an image and they are less concerned about exposure (although they want the right exposure) than the amateur, who seems to spend more time worrying about lens openings and shutter speed combinations than making the picture.

On any trip, your camera should be ready at all times. The so-called everready case that protects the camera is really a "never-ready" case. You'll miss more photographs keeping your camera under wraps. All you need is a strap to hold your camera around your neck. It doesn't have to be in a case and probably shouldn't be.

Cameras and Lenses

The 35mm camera system is the answer for the traveling photographer. It is relatively light, compact, and you can pack enough gear in a box that fits under an airplane seat to handle any photographic assignment in the world. Most people prefer the SLR (single lens reflex) models, but there are still quite a few serious photographers who insist on rangefinder cameras. This is a matter of personal preference, but the important point is to build an interchangeable system. Think of cameras in terms of bodies and consider the lenses separately.

A friend of ours maintains that everyone should have two of everything. We're not certain where he draws the line, but we're convinced his advice at least applies to camera bodies. If you're going to travel in the outdoor world and remote areas, you cannot get by with less, assuming you are serious about your photography. The exception, of course, is the backpacker who must consider every ounce of weight.

A second camera body serves many purposes. You don't always have to have it on your person, but as long as it's on the trip with you, it's a backup unit. If something is going to fail, you can bet it will happen in the most remote region. Without a second camera body, your picture making could come to an abrupt end. The second camera also enables you to enjoy a degree of flexibility when shooting. You can have one lens on the first camera and a different lens on the second camera. You might also elect to load one with a medium-speed color film and the other with high-speed color film or black and white. Even if you use the same film in both cameras, you can continue photographing at the height of the action should you run out of film in one camera, by switching to the other camera.

Lenses that are interchangeable between bodies are a great advantage. If you have two different makes of cameras or models, you will have to carry duplicate lenses for each one and thus lose one of the main advantages of a system.

The lenses you select are a matter of personal preference, but there are some guidelines that may be helpful. Most photographers buy a camera with a normal lens, because it comes that way. If you substitute a 55mm or 60mm macro lens for the normal lens, you gain the advantage of close-up photography without sacrificing normal photography. This is invaluable for the fisherman, hunter, naturalist, bird watcher, and outdoor enthusiast. That macro lens lets you move up close and fill the frame with smaller objects or parts of larger things. Imagine looking at a full-screen photograph of two tiny eggs in a nest or the fly pattern that the trout rose to or some wildflowers that were particularly abundant. The uses for the macro are limitless and they add a new dimension to your outdoor photography. At the same time, you can capture any normal scene by racking back the focusing ring on the lens. It will give you the flexibility you've been looking for.

If you were limited to only three lenses and you chose the macro for the first one, what would you select for the other two? Again you can argue the point forever, but looking at the broad spectrum, your best bet would be a 28mm wide angle and a 135mm telephoto. The 28mm is wide enough to work the cockpit of a boat or a small skiff, and it can do a good job anywhere you need the enlarged angle of view. A 35mm wide angle is too close to the normal lens and a 24mm or 21mm is often too wide.

The 135mm telephoto is a medium lens and it is usually very sharp. You can use it for closeups of people's faces, shooting from a distance so you don't have to poke a camera at someone or so that you can capture the picture without the subject knowing you are taking it. This lens also lets you reach out for other things and it's as long a lens as you need for jumping fish. The trick to photographing jumping fish is to get them close to the boat. You just can't hold many longer lenses steady on the water.

If you are interested in wildlife photography, you should have a long telephoto. A 400mm lens can handle most situations nicely. Lenses longer than that require a tripod almost all the time, and

Use the macro lens as a normal lens or to make extreme closeups.

lenses between 200mm and 400mm are nice to have, but if you are limited to one lens, take the 400mm. It goes without saying that you must have a gunstock or shoulder pod to use a 400mm effectively. The greatest danger is camera movement and you cannot always shoot at high shutter speeds when an animal takes refuge under a bush where you may lose two or three stops.

The gunstock also helps you to get on target quickly and to keep the camera and lens steady. You can brace it against a tree or across the hood of a Land Rover if need be. For a camera safari in Africa, a gunstock-mounted 400mm is

essential to good animal close-ups and portraits.

You may not want to invest in a 400mm if you are merely going on safari to view game and are not a serious wildlife photographer. Should that be the case, you might use a 2X tele-extender with a 200mm lens or 135mm lens. Understand that you will be sacrificing quality with this set up, but it may be better than not getting any photographs at all.

It may seem enjoyable to buy new equipment before a major trip, but, if you do, buy it well in advance so that you have a chance to become familiar with it. As soon as you get the gear, run some test rolls and

Gunstock keeps camera steady and on target.

just handle the camera and lenses so that it becomes second nature to you. The battered-looking bodies of a pro's cameras got that way because they were used over and over again.

Regardless how long you've owned your equipment, you should run a test roll of film through it before a major trip. Cameras have a habit of quitting without warning and, even though it worked the last time you used it, it may not be functioning perfectly right now.

Film

Film is the cheapest and most important commodity you take on your trip. If you have to limit your picture-taking to keep from running out of film, you're going to miss out on the best chances of the trip. The basic rule is to take at least *twice* as much film as you think you could possibly use. When it comes to film, you should be totally self-sufficient the moment you leave home, and you should not depend on buying film anywhere on your itinerary. If you can get film in other countries, it may not be fresh and you can bet it's going to be expensive. Buy your film at home before you leave and buy enough of it.

The types of film you select depend on your personal preferences and, to some extent, on the type of photography you will be doing and the lenses you are using. The important point is to stick to one or two types of film and learn to use them correctly. After a while, you begin to develop a feel for exposure and you can sense if the meter isn't telling all it knows.

For black and white photography, Tri-X is perhaps the best all around choice. It is a fast film and works well under a wide range of light conditions. You may get more detail and a little less grain with a slower film, but in the total analysis, the advantages of the slower film don't always outweigh the disadvantages. Remember that you need fast shutter speeds to capture action and that slower lenses require faster film.

Most photography today involves color film and the majority of 35mm camera enthusiasts prefer positive transparencies that can be projected on a screen. For most photography on a trip, you need a film with an ASA 64 unless you are making scenics under good light conditions. Kodak has a new film called Kodachrome 64 that boasts most of the attributes of the old Kodachrome II (which is no longer manufactured), but has an ASA 64. The old Kodachrome II has been replaced with another ASA 25 film called Kodachrome 25.

Kodak Ektachrome X has long been the choice of many outdoor photographers. Many of these users will try Kodachrome 64 and will probably decide on one of the two films for most of their work.

There are times when light levels are low and when you need every bit of film speed you can get. It's always a good idea on any trip to carry a few rolls of High Speed Ektachrome with you (ASA 160). If need be, this film can be pushed to ASA 400 and processed for the faster speed. Lenses such as a 400mm that may be an f6.8 or f6.3 often require a fast film so that you can use enough shutter speed to prevent camera motion.

The best way to carry film is to remove the cannisters from the cardboard packaging and keep them in a plastic bag (open at the top and not sealed) in your hand luggage. The tops of the cannisters should be color coded to help you identify the type of film instantly. There are various ways to do this. You can use spray paint or felt-tip markers or you can use gummed labels (on which you can write the expiration date). You can use red for High Speed Ektachrome, blue for Ektachrome X, black for Kodachrome 64, and green for Tri-X (or any combination of colors that appeals to you).

If you use gummed labels, buy those that are 5/8's or 3/8's of an inch in diameter. Write the expiration date of the film on the label *before* you peel it off and paste it on the cannister. Then, after you expose the film and return it to the cannister, peel the label off and stick it on the bottom of the cannister. That way, you won't make a mistake and pick up a cannister of exposed film. You may want to change film in a hurry or just put a couple of fresh rolls in your pocket and a mistake with exposed film can be frustrating.

Everybody knows how to load cameras properly, but somehow, there are always those folks who return home to find that the best pictures they thought they made were on a roll that didn't advance in the camera. When they go to rewind the roll after 36 exposures, they crank the rewind knob three times and feel the film slip off the sprocket.

There's a simple and foolproof method of loading a 35mm camera rapidly. Start by opening the back and advancing the film advance lever until the shutter is cocked. This keeps the take-up spool from moving. Take the tab on the film and seat it in the slot on the take-up spool. Depress the shutter release and start to advance the film, watching to insure that the teeth on the sprockets engage the holes in the film. Note that the film cartridge is still in your hand and has not been placed in the camera.

Once the film is engaged, drop the cartridge in the other side of the camera. Use the film advance lever to take up any slack. If the film is engaged in the sprocket holes and looks securely fastened to the take-up spool, close the back of the camera. Before you do anything else, lift up the rewind knob and turn it in the "rewind" direction until you feel the tension. Now, as you advance the film, watch the rewind knob. If it isn't turning backward each time you move the film advance lever, the film is not advancing. It's that simple. Make sure, however, that the rewind lever is tight. Otherwise, you won't see it advance.

On any trip, it's always best to carry 36-exposure rolls of film instead of 20-exposure rolls. You have the capacity for almost twice the number of photographs in the same size cartridge and it doesn't take any more room in your suitcase or hand luggage. And, don't be skimpy when you take pictures. If a picture is worth taking, it's probably a good idea to take more than one.

Film and X-Ray Machines

It's no secret that a certain amount of radiation will fog films. However, a little radiation can affect the film. For one thing, it can upset the color balance or cause the film to be a stop or two off. That's enough to make the pictures worthless.

Most airports in the United States now use x-ray machines as part of their security check for the hand luggage of all passengers. There are signs that inform the uneducated public that the machine will not harm film and, perhaps in most cases it won't if the machine does not malfunction and if it is operated as the manufacturer intended it to be.

Interestingly, Kodak, who has studied the effects of these machines, will not issue a blanket endorsement of them. Instead, they carefully word their statements to leave some doubt. You may also want to consider that radiation has a cumulative effect and if you carry the same film through several check points, you may exceed the limitations.

The best procedure is to insist that your camera and film be inspected visually and that it not be allowed to pass under the x-ray machine. In most cases, you will be accommodated promptly and quietly if you insist on visual inspection a second time after you are told that the machine is totally harmless to film. There are a few places where you may have to request supervisory personnel for the inspection, but it's worth the investment in time and effort.

Outside of the United States, security officers of most countries will comply with your request to visually inspect hand luggage.

However, in some places, x-ray machines are used to examine all of the luggage that will be carried in the baggage compartments of the airplane. It's not the best place to pack film. If you do put film in a suitcase, put a warning label on the outside saying that there is undeveloped film inside and to protect it from x-ray and heat. That, of course, doesn't mean your warning will be heeded.

What Equipment to Take

There are many factors influencing the amount of photographic equipment you take on any trip, beginning with the type of photography you hope to do and where you are going. In addition to two camera bodies and assorted lenses (for most trips), you may want to consider filters, flash units, tripods, exposure meter, and similar items.

The first requirement is that you can carry all that gear. Camera equipment should be with you all the time and should not be shipped as baggage or remain out of your sight. With careful planning, you can put a great deal in an aluminum case that fits beneath your airplane seat. That doesn't mean that you have to carry everything with you once you reach your destination. It's a good idea to carry a lightweight shoulder bag with strap for equipment once you arrive at the lodge.

If most of your photography is going to involve a telephoto over 400mm or 500mm, you may have to carry a sturdy tripod. And, you may need one if you are going to take a lot of close-ups in the field. For most purposes, however, you can get by without this cumbersome item of equipment. It may be nice to have, but it's tough to lug around. Instead, build a shoulder stock for your long lens and make use of gadgets such as a minipod of some type that has three short legs and can be braced against a wall or your chest or a tree.

In remote regions, strobe units that have rechargeable batteries must be considered seriously. If you don't have the facilities to recharge the unit, there's not much point in taking it. The serious outdoor photographer should have small units with replaceable batteries as well as the nickel-cadmium variety. Filters are a matter of choice, but if you work on the water or around snow, you may find a polarizing filter exceptionally useful. Polarizers, by the way, are the best haze filter you can find and they are excellent for making photographs from airplanes. An extra exposure meter is nice to have, but not absolutely necessary.

There is one item that any outdoor photographer should never be without; the plastic bag. Actually, you need at least two sizes of plastic bags in the field—32-gallon garbage-pail liners that can quickly be placed over your camera case to protect it from rain or spray and the smaller, clear plastic type that can be put over your camera in the rain. Put a hole for your lens in the clear plastic bag and you can make some great photos in the rain.

Tips On Making Photos

Photo possibilities on any trip start even before you leave and you should be alert to them. You may want to take some packing, preparation, and departure shots. The point to remember above all others is that you can't take good photographs if you're not willing to work at it. Experience will eventually convince you that when you have to debate with yourself whether or not you should take a particular picture, the answer is invariably yes. It may be troublesome to pull a camera out, but you can be certain that you will regret more photos that you didn't take than those you did.

Following the same line of thinking, if you want your pictures to be above the ordinary, you can't follow the crowd. At some of the so-called scenic wonders of this world, there are well-worn paths to the spot where everyone puts a camera to his eye and clicks the shutter. That spot may seem like the best location at the moment, but with a little more thought, you may be able to come up with a unique camera angle.

To do this, you have to be willing to walk or climb. Perhaps you'll have to walk to a higher piece of ground or crawl around some bushes to get to an even better vista. You can bet that most photographers won't do this and that is what will make the difference in the pictures you take.

There's an adage among photographers that says, "Shoot it wrong and then shoot it right." Too often, we tend to procrastinate, deluding ourselves that we will return when the lighting is better or waiting to recreate some action rather than attempting to shoot it live first. The adage tells us to get something on film at the earliest opportunity, even though it may not be the picture we are seeking. Then, if everything is perfect and we have the chance, go back and shoot it the right way. More often than not, the first pictures will be the only ones we have to show for our efforts. To a photographer, there is no such thing as later or tomorrow. Take the picture the instant you recognize the potential and then come back to get the better one. It could rain tomorrow.

Learning to hold a camera steady may sound basic, but not doing so causes more fuzzy pictures than you can imagine. Equally important, you must also learn to hold a camera level. Water does not run up hill on the ocean and gravity in other surroundings hates to be defied. It's easy to do when you have plenty of time to take the photograph, but if you're waiting for a trophy fish to come out of the water, you only have a second or two to put it all together. The important thing is to be aware of the typical shortcomings.

The key to action photography, of course, is anticipation. You must decide where and how the action will take place and then place yourself in position to make the photograph when the action occurs. Grab shots are wonderful if you get lucky, but good action photography is more often the result of careful planning and positioning. Not only must you position yourself, but you should pre-set and pre-focus your camera as well. Then, when it happens, you merely have to compose the picture and trip the shutter.

There are a lot of great pictures that can be taken from airplanes if you are alert to them. You should position yourself on the shady side, which means that the sun will be on your subject. Use a haze filter or a polarizer if you have enough light to cut down on glare and haze. The vibration in an airplane is the problem and that means you should use the fastest shutter speed you can. Hold the camera as steady as possible and near the window or windshield, but don't let the camera, your arms, or your body touch the side of the plane or the window. That's all there is to it. You'll be amazed at some of the pleasing photographs you can take from the window of the plane. They are great for showing the terrain and for showing transition in a slide lecture from one location to another.

Working in the outdoors isn't always the easiest type of photography, especially when you are trying to capture wildlife or fish on film. There are situations where you have all kinds of time and other instances where speed counts. As an example, if your camera is set on the basic exposure for a frontlit subject and you have to swing quickly to a sidelit subject, open up one stop. If you continue your swing to a backlit subject, open up two stops. This is a rule of thumb, but when speed counts you're going to be close and you'll get the picture.

If you participate in a game-viewing safari, there are a few suggestions that might be helpful. You'll find that if you focus on the eye of an animal, the whole creature will appear in focus when you view the results. But, if the eye is out of focus, the animal will seem fuzzy, even though the rest of the animal is razor sharp.

You always have to be ready to take photographs in animal country. That means you should pre-set your camera for the logical expectation. Consider the light conditions and focus for a medium range that will give you a depth of field to infinity. Animals are often sensitive to sudden movement. You'll find that if you move slowly, you won't spook them as badly. They may move off, but it won't be in a hurry. A lot of animals will try to put some type of cover in front of them and then turn around for another look at the intruder. Anticipate this and be ready. At the same time recognize that you may have to open up two stops to properly expose that animal once it reaches the shade under the tree or behind the bush.

Photography is a technique for individual expression and the perfect way to capture the excitement of any outdoor adventure. The pictures you take will reflect your interest in the trip and how you interpreted the things you saw. They will jog your memory for years to come, and the only regret you will ever have is not taking ten times as many photographs on the trip. Remember that film is the cheapest commodity you have. Use plenty of it and preserve the memories.

CHOOSING AND USING BINOCULARS

Binoculars add to the richness of any outdoor experience and a quality pair can be a lifetime investment that will enhance your observations on land or sea. With reasonable care, a fine optical instrument does not wear out and will render superb service year after year.

The problem of selecting the right pair of binoculars for your use can be simplified if you are willing to follow a few basic rules. And, with just a bit of semi-technical data, you can become somewhat of an expert in choosing a good pair of binoculars.

Any pair of binoculars is a compromise. There are advantages and disadvantages and, like bartering in a native bazaar, you try to obtain the best combination of advantages. If you can define the main use to which your binoculars will be put, you almost have the answer as to model and style. As we investigate each feature, think in terms of how it would apply to your needs.

Magnification or Power

Each pair of binoculars is designated by a pair of numbers such as 7 x 35, 8 x 30, 10 x 40, etc. The first number (7X, 8X, 10X, etc.) refers to magnification. An object viewed through a 7X pair of glasses is seven times larger than you would see it with the unaided eye. Magnification is also called "power" and a 7X magnification is often referred to as 7 power.

It's important to understand that quality does not improve just because the magnification is increased. There are both advantages and disadvantages to increased magnification. If you can hold glasses of higher magnification steady, the enlarged image may be an advantage, but it is not easy to handhold 10 power glasses unless you can brace your arms or body. If the glasses move, they will magnify the movement of the image and your eyes won't be able to focus on the image. That means that things will look fuzzy. Lower power is more forgiving for movement and that should be considered if you are going to use the glasses in a boat, from a car or other moving conveyance, or intend to sweep the glasses to follow action.

The second number in the designation of binoculars (7 x 35, 8 x 30, etc.) is the diameter of the objective lenses measured in millimeters. It has no relation to field of view, but it does affect relative brightness as we'll see in a moment.

Field of View

Field of view is nothing more than how much you can see through the binoculars at a given distance without moving them. It can be expressed as an angle, but it is more generally noted as a linear measurement in feet at 1,000 yards. Major manufacturers now offer various degrees of wide angle binoculars in addition to the standard models. You can, for example, get a pair of 7 x 35 binoculars with a field of view of 420' at 1000 yards or 520' at 1,000 yards or 578' at 1,000 yards, all from the same manufacturer.

It is somewhat easier to locate an object if the glasses offer a wide field of view, because you see

more without moving the binoculars. You also do not have to swing the binoculars as quickly to follow action.

If you compare two glasses of the same design, the one with higher magnification will have the narrower field of view. Understand that there are special wide angle glasses and you can't compare a wide angle pair of binoculars to a standard pair. However, not all manufacturers label their glasses accurately. The best insurance you have is to place your confidence in a reputable brand of binoculars. You can check field of view for yourself by taking two pairs of binoculars of the same magnification and focusing on a distant object that is larger than the area that binoculars cover. Note how much you can see in each one and the pair that spans the wider area has the wider field of view.

There's one other area of caution with which you should be familiar. Edge sharpness and edge brightness are important considerations. A pair of binoculars may have a wide field, but it is achieved at a sacrifice of clear resolution around the edges. This is not true of the better quality and better designed glasses, which are tailored to provide excellent definition out to the extreme edges. When you do look through a pair of glasses, concentrate on edge sharpness. If things get fuzzy toward the edges, look for another pair.

Relative Brightness

When you look through a pair of binoculars, you put your eyes

against the ocular lenses. The objective lenses are the larger lenses on the opposite side of the glasses. If you hold the binoculars at arm's length with the objective lenses pointing at the sky or a bright light and look at the ocular lenses, you will see two bright circles of light which are much smaller than the ocular lenses. This is the amount of light that leaves the binocular and enters your eye. It is technically known as the exit pupil.

Regardless how much light exits from the binoculars, only so much of it will enter the eye. We all know that the pupils in our eyes adjust to the amount of light by expanding and contracting. The pupil opens in dim light to allow more light to enter, and closes down in bright light to limit the amount of light that can enter.

Exit pupil can be expressed in millimeters as the diameter of the circle of light leaving the binoculars. The basic formula is to divide the magnification into the diameter of the objective lens. That means that the exit pupil of 7 x 35 binoculars would be 5mm (35mm divided by 7). There is another measurement or guide number known as relative brightness, which is nothing more than the exit pupil squared (in our example, 5 times 5 or 25).

A great deal of research has been done on pupil diameter of the human eye and it has been found that it does *not* vary with the individual but remains constant. Regardless of how bright it may be, your pupil will not contract below 2.5 mm, and in total darkness it will be about 7 mm. At dawn or dusk, pupil diameter is approximately 5 mm and it may contract to 3.5 mm on a dark day.

Any pair of binoculars with an exit pupil of 5mm (relative brightness of 25) can be used effectively from dawn to dusk., Your eyes just won't accept any more light. At night, if the exit pupil is 7mm (relative brightness around 50), you've reached the maximum. If you are going to use binoculars after dark, you need a pair with an exit pupil of 7 mm to gain maximum effectiveness.

A number of manufacturers list the diameter of the exit pupil in their literature for your convenience.

Coating

Most people don't realize that there is a loss of light transmission between every surface of glass and the air around it. If you wear eyeglasses, for example, about 8% of the light is lost through reflection before it reaches your eyes. The same concept applies to binoculars. Every time you have an optic, you lose between 4% and 6% of light on each side of the lens.

Modern binoculars may have as many as twelve lenses in them and that means that half of the light may be lost before it ever reaches your eye. To improve light transmission and reduce reflection, lenses today are coated with a molecular layer of special metallic salt. Their coating increases light transmission by at least 50%.

The coating, if done properly, has even more value. You must be concerned with image contrast or quality as well as brightness. Coated optics eliminate the flat and

hazy images and produce crisp detail in which dark areas are dark and light areas are light. It is a waste of money to buy binoculars that do not have properly coated lenses.

It is even more important to coat the internal lenses than the outside of the objective lenses and ocular lenses. If a manufacturer wanted to cut corners, he could merely coat the outside elements. You can check this by holding your binoculars in front of you with a bright light or sky in the background. Look through the larger or objective lens and twist the binoculars until you can see a reflection. Coated lenses show up as purple or blue, while uncoated interior elements will show up as a bright reflection.

Image quality

No matter how much magnification a pair of binoculars has or how much light it transmits, unless the image is sharp, the glasses are virtually useless. When you handle a pair of binoculars in a store, you can quickly check out some of the more significant factors in this area. As an example, look at a building in the distance or something else with straight lines or right angles. If the edges of these lines bulge inward or bend outward, the glasses have distortion and are best left right there.

Check the edge sharpness again. Both the edges and the center of the image should be crisp at the same time. If you focus on the center and the edges appear fuzzy, or if you focus on the edges and the center moves out of focus,

the glasses have an uncorrected curvature.

If there is a brick wall nearby or something with a pattern, use this to check the binoculars for overall sharpness and distortion. A newspaper makes an ideal test plate indoors or outside. Tape the paper to a wall and then move back until you can't quite read the small type. Try various pairs of binoculars of the same magnification and the one that makes the letters appear sharpest should have the best image.

When you perform the exit pupil test by holding the glasses at arm's length with the objective lenses pointing toward a light source, look closely at the circle of light in each ocular lens. In good quality glasses, each circle of light is crisp with sharply defined edges. If the edges of the circle aren't perfectly round or if there is a grayish area, look for another pair of glasses.

If you wear eyeglasses to correct your vision, keep them on when you try out different binoculars. Note that some types will restrict your field of view when you are wearing glasses. There are other makes, however, that use specially designed rubber eyecups to enable the eyeglass wearer to enjoy a full field of view.

Focus and Binoculars

For most outdoor activities, center focusing models are superior to individual focus. Center focus binoculars have a focusing wheel on the hinge post and you can also focus the right eyepiece. If you only intend to view items beyond 50 feet or more away from you, an individual focus model may suit your needs. Since each eyepiece must be focused separately, it is inconvenient if you have to change the focus in the field. Normally, the center focus types are a better choice.

In focusing your binoculars, the first step is to set the hinge to fit the distance between your eyes (interpupillary distance). Bend the binoculars at the hinge until the two images superimpose and you see one, clear, crisp image. It is always best to set the focus when viewing a clearly defined object such as a sign. Close your right eye or cover the right objective lens and, using only your left eye, turn the focusing wheel until you see the object clearly. Now, close your left eye and turn the adjustable eyecup for the right eye until the object comes into focus. Your glasses are set and all further focusing is done with the focusing wheel. Make a note of the individual eyepiece setting, so that you can reset it at any time without going through this procedure.

Some Additional Thoughts

You now know how to determine the quality of binoculars and how the various factors can affect your use of the glasses. There are a few other considerations. Perhaps the primary one is size and weight. If you're going to use them in the field, do a lot of walking, carry them where weight is a problem, require something small enough to pack easily or fit in a pocket, your choice of binoculars will be limited. This is a major consideration and most outdoorsmen prefer the lighter, smaller models.

Unless you have some way of holding them rigid, anything over 10 power is going to cause problems and, for general field work, anything over 8 power should be considered carefully. The most popular size binoculars are 7 x 35, simply because they are good compromise without any serious negative imbalances.

When you shop for binoculars, consider the quality, magnification, field of view, light gathering ability, construction, weight, size, and focusing. Get the best compromise and you should have endless years of enjoyment.

CONSERVATION ORGANIZATIONS

We thought you might appreciate having a list of some of the leading environmental and outdoor organizations, and getting an idea of what they do. Each focuses on different kinds of issues—seeing that trout streams are clear and clean, for instance, that mountain trails are well-maintained, that the wetlands are preserved, that air pollution is reduced—but they share a common devotion to our national wildlife and wilderness heritage. Which one you might care to support depends on your own interests and activities, but your concern and participation can make a difference. Many of these organizations—the Sierra Club and the Audubon Society are outstanding examples—offer their members informative and beautifully illustrated publications which will interest you and your children and keep you in touch with the outdoor world throughout

the year. They also offer all kinds of special programs, trips, book clubs and charter flights.

American Forestry Association, The
1319 18th Street, N.W.,
Washington, D.C. 20036
(202-467-5810)
Objective is advancement of intelligent management and use of forests, soil, water, wildlife and all other natural resources. Seeks to create an enlightened public appreciation of these resources and the part they play in the social and economic life of the nation. Created 1875. Publishes *American Forests.*

American League of Anglers
810 18th Street, N.W.,
Washington, D.C. 20006
(202-347-7475)

A political action organization whose motto is ''Fish don't vote . . . fishermen do,'' American League of Anglers was formed to do the lobbying that non-profit fishing organizations cannot do and to fight pollution, real estate encroachments on fishing waters, stream diversions, and the pressures of foreign fleets on United States waters.

Appalachian Mountain Club
5 Joy Street, Boston, Mass. 02108
(617-523-0636)
Sponsors program of recreational service in the northeastern mountains, including trail and shelter maintenance in eight states; publishes guidebooks and maps, operates nine-unit public hut system, conducts varied activity and educational programs for members and non-members. Membership: 17,000. Founded

Nonprofit, nonpolitical membership corporation, organized to perpetuate wild ducks and other wild waterfowl on the North American continent, principally by development, preservation, restoration management, and maintenance of wetland areas on the Canadian primary breeding grounds, which produce the majority of continental waterfowl. Establishes, promotes, assists, and contributes to conservation, restoration and management of waterfowl habitat. Membership: 100,000. Organized 1937. Publishes *Ducks Unlimited Magazine*

Hudson River Sloop Restoration, Inc.
Market St., Poughkeepsie,
N.Y. 12601
(914-454-7912)
Formed in 1966 to fight pollution of the Hudson River, it launched the Clearwater, a replica of the cargo sloops once common on the Hudson, and it now sails the sloop on the Hudson and Long Island Sound, monitoring the water, running programs in public education, community awareness and sailing. Members are invited to sail on the *Clearwater* or to serve as crew. Publishes the *North River Navigator*.

International Association of Game, Fish and Conservation Commissioners
1709 New York Avenue, N.W.,
Washington D.C. 20006
(202-872-8866)
An association joining of each state or territory of the United States, each Province of Canada, the Commonwealth of Puerto Rico, the United States Government, the Dominion Government of Canada

1876. Publishes: *Appalachia, Appalachian Bulletin.*

Appalachian Trail Conference
P.O. Box 236, Harpers Ferry,
W. Va. 25425
(304-535-6331)
Coordinates maintenance, preservation and general welfare of the Appalachian Trail, a 2,000- mile wilderness footpath generally following the crest of the Appalachian Mountains from Maine to Georgia. Prepares and distributes trail guidebooks. Publishes *Appalachian Trailway News.*

Ducks Unlimited, Inc.
Box 66300, Chicago, Ill. 60666
(312-299-3334)

and each government of a country located in the Western Hemisphere as well as individual Associate members whose principal objective is conservation, protection and management of wildlife and related natural resources. Publishes *Annual Proceedings; Newsletter.*

International Atlantic Salmon Foundation, The
P.O. Box 429, St. Andrews,
N.B., Canada
506-529-3818; 425 Park Avenue,
New York, N.Y. 10022
A nonprofit research and educational organization dedicated to the conservation and wise management of the Atlantic Salmon and its environment. Directs and supports many vital programs in areas of education, public information, research and international cooperation. Founded 1968. Publishes *I.A.S.F. Newsletter, Special Publication Series.*

Izaak Walton League
of America, The
1800 North Kent Street, Suite 806,
Arlington, Va. 22209
(703-528-1818)
Promotes means and opportunities for educating the public to conserve, maintain, protect and restore the soil, forest, water and other natural resources of the United States and encourages the enjoyment and wholesome utilization of those resources. Membership: 56,000.

National Audubon Society
950 Third Avenue, New York,
N.Y. 10022
(212-832-3200)
Its purposes are to promote the conservation of wildlife and the natural environment and to

educate man regarding his relationship with, and his place within, the natural environment as an ecological system. Founded 1905. Publishes *Audubon; Audubon Leader; American Birds.*

National Recreation and Park Association
1601 North Kent Street, Arlington, Va. 22209
(703-525-0606)
A nonprofit service, education and research organization dedicated to the improvement of park and recreation leadership, programs and facilities. The Association fosters public understanding that leisure programs and environments are indispensable to the well-being of a nation and its citizens. Membership: 17,000. Publishes: *Parks and Recreation Magazine; Communique; Journal of Leisure Research; Therapeutic Recreation Journal; A Guide to Books on Parks, Recreation and Leisure; Washington Action Report.*

National Rifle Association of America
1600 Rhode Island Avenue, N.W., Washington, D.C. 20036
(202-783-6505)
Educates and trains reputable citizens in the safe and efficient handling of firearms; fosters the conservation, better management and wise use of our renewable wildlife resources; promotes social welfare and public safety, law and order, good sportsmanship, and the National Defense through programs of Hunter Safety Training, Home Firearms Safety, Junior and Senior Marksmanship, and Wildlife Research; maintains liason with governmental and

private conservation organizations and state fish and game departments. Membership: 1,000,000. Organized 1871. Publishes *The American Rifleman.*

National Wildlife Federation, The
1412 16th Street, N.W.,
Washington D.C. 20036
202-483-1550
To create and encourage an awareness among the people of this nation of the need for wise use and proper management of those resources of the earth upon which the lives and welfare of man depend; . . . the soils, plant life and the wildlife. Organized 1936. Publishes*National Wildlife, International Wildlife, Conservation News, Ranger Rick's Nature Magazine.*

North American Wildlife Foundation
709 Wire Building, Washington, D.C. 20005
(202-347-1775)
Helps to sponsor wildlife research, through cooperating organizations and institutions, into all phases of natural resource conservation, restoration and management.

Sierra Club
1050 Mills Tower, San Francisco, California 94104
(415-981-8634)
Works to protect and conserve the natural resources of the Sierra Nevada, the United States, and the world; undertakes and reports on scientific and educational studies concerning all aspects of man's environment and the natural ecosystems of the world; organizes programs to educate the people of the United States and the world to the need to preserve and restore the quality of that environment and

the integrity of these ecosystems. Forty-three chapters coast-to-coast. The club's nonprofit programs include wilderness outings, whitewater trips, skiing, mountaineering, knapsacking, films, exhibits, conferences, 14 huts and lodges, a library, and publishing. Founded 1892 by John Muir. Publishes *Sierra Club Bulletin, National News Report.*

Sport Fishing Institute
Suite 801, 608 13th Street, N.W.,
Washington, D.C. 20005
(202-783-0668)
Aims to improve sport fishing through fish conservation research, education and service based on the philosophy that "the quality of fishing reflects the quality of living;" helps protect aquatic ecosystems by assisting fish conservationists in developing new and improved fisheries research management programs designed to protect aquatic environments and enhance vital fisheries resources. Incorporated 1949. Publishes *S.F.I. Bulletin.*

Theodore Gordon Flyfishers, Inc.
24 East 39th Street, New York,
N.Y. 10016
(212-697-5300)
Named after the "father" of American fly-fishing, the club fights for cleaner waters by training teams of pollution detectors who test rivers and streams all over the U.S. each month. Was instrumental in creating "no-kill" sections on the waterways. Meets each Tuesday for luncheons in New York City at the Williams Club.

Trout Unlimited
4260 East Evans Avenue,
Denver, Colorado 80222

(303-757-7144)
A nonprofit, nonpolitical, conservation-minded membership organization, formed to preserve clearwaters and to perpetuate and improve high-quality fishing by supporting and encouraging the proper management of water and trout populations, based upon biological and synecological facts. Publishes *Trout Magazine.*

Wetlands for Wildlife, Inc.
114 South Main Street,
P.O. Box 147, Mayville,
Wis. 53050
(414-387-4878)
Advocates and participates in promotion, preservation and acquisition of wetlands and wildlife habitat in the United States which will be transferred to federal, state or country agencies exclusively for public purposes. Publishes *Thirsty Times.*

Wilderness Society, The
1901 Pennsylvania Avenue, N.W.,
Washington D.C. 20006
(202-239-2732)
National conservation organization, formed to secure preservation of the wilderness, carry on an educational program concerning the value of wilderness and how it may best be used and preserved in the public interest, make and encourage scientific studies of wilderness, and mobilize cooperation in resisting its invasion. Membership: 80,000. Publishes *The Living Wilderness.*

Wildlife Management Institute
709 Wire Building,
Washington D.C. 20005
(202-347-1774)
National, nonprofit, private membership organization, supported by industries, groups

and individuals, promoting better use of natural resources for the welfare of the nation. Publishes *Outdoor News Bulletin; Transactions North American Wildlife and Natural Resources Conference.*

Wildlife Society, The
Suite S-176, 3905 Wisconsin Avenue, N.W., Washington, D.C. 20016
(202-363-2435)
Association of those professionally employed in the biological or related fields of wildlife conservation. Aims to develop and promote sound stewardship of wildlife resources and the environments upon which wildlife and man depend; undertakes an active role in preventing man-induced environmental degradation; increases awareness and appreciation of wildlife values; and seeks the highest standards in all activities of the wildlife profession. Membership: 7,000. Publishes: *Journal of Wildlife Management, Wildlife Society Bulletin, Wildlife Monographs.*

World Wildlife Fund,
Suite 619, 910 17th Street, N.W.,
Washington, D.C. 20006
(202-296-6114)
Private, tax-exempt international conservation organization supporting a program to save threatened and endangered wildlife and natural areas. Makes grants for land acquisition, habitat protection and maintenance, and scientific ecological research around the globe. WWF includes 24 national affiliates, with international headquarters located in Morges, Switzerland. Supporters: 45,000; Established: 1961.

PLANNING YOUR OUTDOOR YEAR

A&F TRIP PLANners
Recollections
Outdoor Travel Specialists
It's Your Book Now

A & F TRIP PLANner

Turn to this section when you first begin to think about having an outdoor adventure. Fill in and check off the information as you put the trip together. After completing your TRIP PLANner, make copies for your office & home and for other persons who may require this information, including yourself if you do not plan to take your Outdoor Diary with you.

---

1. PURPOSE OF TRIP AND DESTINATION

Dates: From: To:

2. TRAVEL AGENT

Name

Address

Tel. No.

---

3. PLACE TO STAY (Main location)

Address

Tel. No./Cable/Telex

Manager's Name

U.S. Contact

Reservation   Yes ☐ No☐

Rate $

Deposit $

Balance $

---

4. TRANSPORTATION

	Destination	Airline	Tel.	Airport	Flt. No.	Depart	Arrive
Going							
Return							

Baggage Allowance   Lbs. Over   Special packing

---

5. AUTO RENTAL

At destination   Company   Reser. No.

---

6. ENTRY REQUIREMENTS

Passport   Visa

Vaccinations & Inoculations

Duty free personal allowance

Foreign currency

In	Out

---

7. CORRESPONDENCE

Name   Address   Notations

8. EQUIPMENT TO BE TAKEN

	Serial Number
Item	Registered Customs
	Special packing

Fishing

Hunting

Other

Camera

Lenses

Radio

Tape recorder

Binoculars

Other

9. MEDICAL

Allergies	Blood type
Prescription medicines:	Special medical information

Anti-histamines; anti-biotics:

Eyeglass prescription

Physician's name

Address	Tel.

in case of emergency notify

13. SUGGESTED TRAVEL SUPPLIES

Batteries for camera, radio, etc.

Knife with blades, can opener, screw driver, corkscrew

Nail Clipper

Scissors

Folding umbrella

Thermometer

Folding knife, fork, spoon

Extra comb

Needles, thread, buttons

Spot remover, detergent

Pen, pencil, pad, envelopes, stationery, scotch tape, safety pins, rubber bands

Aspirin

Tissues

Other

10. CREDIT CARDS

Company	Card No.	Notify in case of loss

11. TRAVELERS CHECKS

Numbers

Notify in case of loss

12. SHOPPING FOR FAMILY AND FRIENDS

Person	Shoe size	Dress size	Shirt size	Suit size	Other items

RECOLLECTIONS

On these pages you can note the high points of your trip,
the things you'd want to recall if you went that way again,
the comments made by your companions and even your guide.
There's space for some sketches (try pencil or pen)
and to paste in a photograph or two.
Use these pages, you'll enjoy reading them in years to come.

A & F TRIP PLANner

Turn to this section when you first begin to think about having an outdoor adventure. Fill in and check off the information as you put the trip together. After completing your TRIP PLANner, make copies for your office & home and for other persons who may require this information, including yourself if you do not plan to take your Outdoor Diary with you.

1. PURPOSE OF TRIP AND DESTINATION

Dates: From: To:

2. TRAVEL AGENT

Name

Address

Tel. No.

3. PLACE TO STAY (Main location)

Address

Tel. No./Cable/Telex

Manager's Name

U.S. Contact

Reservation   Yes ☐   No☐

Rate $

Deposit $

Balance $

4. TRANSPORTATION

	Destination	Airline	Tel.	Airport	Flt. No.	Depart	Arrive
Going							
Return							

Baggage Allowance   Lbs. Over   Special packing

5. AUTO RENTAL

At destination   Company   Reser. No.

6. ENTRY REQUIREMENTS

Passport   Visa

Vaccinations & Inoculations

Duty free
personal allowance

Foreign currency

	In	Out

7. CORRESPONDENCE

Name   Address   Notations

8. EQUIPMENT TO BE TAKEN

Item

Serial Number
Registered Customs
Special packing

Fishing

Hunting

Other

Camera

Lenses

Radio

Tape recorder

Binoculars

Other

9. MEDICAL

Allergies   Blood type

Prescription medicines: Special medical information

Anti-histamines; anti-biotics:

Eyeglass prescription

Physician's name

Address   Tel.

in case of emergency notify

13. SUGGESTED TRAVEL SUPPLIES

Batteries for camera, radio, etc.

Knife with blades, can opener,
screw driver, corkscrew

Nail Clipper

Scissors

Folding umbrella

Thermometer

Folding knife, fork, spoon

Extra comb

Needles, thread, buttons

Spot remover, detergent

Pen, pencil, pad, envelopes,
stationery, scotch tape,
safety pins, rubber bands

Aspirin

Tissues

Other

10. CREDIT CARDS

Company   Card No.

Notify in
case of loss

11. TRAVELERS CHECKS

Numbers

Notify in case of loss

12. SHOPPING FOR FAMILY AND FRIENDS

Person	Shoe size	Dress size	Shirt size	Suit size	Other items

RECOLLECTIONS

On these pages you can note the high points of your trip,
the things you'd want to recall if you went that way again,
the comments made by your companions and even your guide.
There's space for some sketches (try pencil or pen)
and to paste in a photograph or two.
Use these pages, you'll enjoy reading them in years to come.

A & F TRIP PLANner

Turn to this section when you first begin to think about having an outdoor adventure. Fill in and check off the information as you put the trip together. After completing your TRIP PLANner, make copies for your office & home and for other persons who may require this information, including yourself if you do not plan to take your Outdoor Diary with you.

---

1. PURPOSE OF TRIP AND DESTINATION

Dates: From: To:

---

2. TRAVEL AGENT

Name

Address

Tel. No.

---

3. PLACE TO STAY (Main location)

Address

Tel. No./Cable/Telex

Manager's Name

U.S. Contact

Reservation   Yes ☐ No☐

Rate $

Deposit $

Balance $

---

4. TRANSPORTATION

	Destination	Airline	Tel.	Airport	Flt. No.	Depart	Arrive
Going							
Return							

Baggage Allowance   Lbs. Over   Special packing

---

5. AUTO RENTAL

At destination   Company   Reser. No.

---

6. ENTRY REQUIREMENTS

Passport   Visa

Vaccinations & Inoculations

	In	Out
Duty free personal allowance		
Foreign currency		

---

7. CORRESPONDENCE

Name   Address   Notations

8. EQUIPMENT TO BE TAKEN

Item   Serial Number
Registered Customs
Special packing

Fishing

Hunting

Other

Camera

Lenses

Radio

Tape recorder

Binoculars

Other

9. MEDICAL

Allergies   Blood type

Prescription medicines: Special medical information

Anti-histamines; anti-biotics:

Eyeglass prescription

Physician's name

Address   Tel.

in case of emergency notify

13. SUGGESTED TRAVEL SUPPLIES

Batteries for camera, radio, etc.

Knife with blades, can opener, screw driver, corkscrew

Nail Clipper

Scissors

Folding umbrella

Thermometer

Folding knife, fork, spoon

Extra comb

Needles, thread, buttons

Spot remover, detergent

Pen, pencil, pad, envelopes, stationery, scotch tape, safety pins, rubber bands

Aspirin

Tissues

Other

10. CREDIT CARDS

Company   Card No.   Notify in case of loss

11. TRAVELERS CHECKS

Numbers

Notify in case of loss

12. SHOPPING FOR FAMILY AND FRIENDS

Person	Shoe size	Dress size	Shirt size	Suit size	Other items

RECOLLECTIONS

On these pages you can note the high points of your trip,
the things you'd want to recall if you went that way again,
the comments made by your companions and even your guide.
There's space for some sketches (try pencil or pen)
and to paste in a photograph or two.
Use these pages, you'll enjoy reading them in years to come.

OUTDOOR TRAVEL SPECIALISTS

One of the surest ways to avoid difficulties and disappointments in arranging travel is to use the services of a qualified travel agent.

However, booking an outdoor adventure—which for most people is not an everyday event—may also not be familiar to every travel agent, and you may want to seek assistance from an outdoor travel specialist. Adventures Unlimited, the travel agency located in Abercrombie & Fitch Co. stores in New York City and San Francisco, has extensive experience in booking outdoor adventures. Adventures Unlimited has booked many of the trips described in this diary and can handle arrangements for all of them. You can reach them at:

ADVENTURES UNLIMITED
19 East 45th Street
New York, New York 10017
Telephone: 212-682-3600   or

220 Post Street
San Francisco, Calif. 94108
Telephone: 415-397-2300

Other outdoor specialists featured in this year's diary were:

ADVENTURE ASSOCIATES
150 S.E. Second Avenue
Miami, Florida 33131
Telephone: 800-327-5781

FISH AND GAME FRONTIERS/
FRONTIERS INTERNATIONAL
Pearce Mill Road
Wexford, Pennsylvania 15090
Telephone: 412-953-1577

HANNS EBENSTEN TRAVEL
55 West 42nd Street
New York, New York 10036
Telephone: 212-354-6634

SAFARI OUTFITTERS
8 South Michigan Avenue
Chicago, Illinois 60603
Telephone: 312-346-9631

In addition to the outdoor opportunities we have listed in this book, these specialists offer a number of other trips that may merit your consideration.

IT'S YOUR BOOK NOW

While the information in this first issue was provided by a handful of outdoor experts, *THE BLAZED TRAIL/Outdoor Diary 1975* is now in the hands of its readers, who together have experienced more outdoor adventures than any handful of experts could ever hope to sample. So if you know of special trips, unique places and things to do in the outdoors and would like to share them with others, the publisher welcomes your suggestions. All letters will receive personal replies.

If your suggestion is used in a subsequent issue of *THE BLAZED TRAIL/Outdoor Diary,* the publisher will send you a copy of that issue with a special "contributor's bookplate" that states your help in providing information. Send your comments and suggestions to Outdoor Year, Inc., P.O. Box 4373, Grand Central Station, New York, N.Y. 10017.

INDEX

Acapulco, 148

Africa, 95-99, 110

Alaska
  hunting, 99
  hunting seasons, 100
  photographic safari, 114

Alvesleben, Baron Werner von, 96

Animal-viewing
  See Game-viewing and
  Photographic safari.

Amazon River cruise, 119

Anthony's Key Resort, 130

Apipe Safaris, 72

Araguaia River Trip, 121

Argentina
  fishing, 46, 71, 72

Arizona, 146, 147

Backpacking, 132, 133, 136, 141, 142

Bahamas, 65

Bailey, Dan, 43, 44

Bailey, John, 140

Baja, California, 138

Banks, Major Mike, 113

Basswood Lake, 136

Barnes, Bill and Linda, 62

Bennett, John, 52

Bermuda, 67

Bermuda Charter Fishing
  Association, 68

Binoculars, 167

Birding, 160
  trips, 111, 115, 118, 121

Black fly, 84

Brazil, 121

Bretton Woods, the Village at,
  151

Cabanas del Caribe, 64

Cajuiles, 150

Camping in Europe, 138

Canada
  fishing, 42, 53, 55
  wingshooting, 92

Canoeing, 133-137
  school, 133

Casa Mar, 62

Cayman Kai, 129

Chalet Club, 128, 129

Chase, Dr. Alston and Diana, 140

Chase Ranch, 140

Chile, 44

Climate, 124

Climbing, 132-133, 140, 142

Clothing, for the outdoors, 124

Club de Patos, 92

Club Pacifico de Panama, 70

Colgate, Steve, 157

Colombia, 73, 94, 116, 120

Conservation
  organizations, 170
  Fish Stamp, 78

Costa Rica, 62

Cozumel, 64

Culp, Bob, 132

Cumilahue River, 44, 79

Daniken, Erich von, 116

De Bell, Garrett, 138

Deep Water Cay Club, 65

Dominican Republic
  golf, 150

Dufflocq, Adrian and Pat, 45

Eagle River, 53

Ecuador, 58, 118

El Dorado Lodge, 73

Engle, Clark, 99, 115

Exum, Glenn, 133

Family vacations, 136

Farleyer House, 89

Faroe Islands, 111

Field Guides, 161

Fish Stamp
  See National Fish Stamp Program

Fishing
  Trout and salmon, 42
  Salt water game fish, 56
  Dorado, 71

Fishing in Europe, 75

Fishing schools, 79

Fishing tackle, 81

Fishing trophies, 83

France
  skiing, 153

Galapagos Islands, 118

Game-viewing, 110, 161
  See also Photographic safaris

Gardner, John, 147

George River, 55

Georgia, 88

Godfrey, Will, 44

Golf, 148-151
  travel with golf clubs, 151

Goose Bay, 53

Grand Teton National Park, 136

Greece
  scuba trip, 130

Greenland
  viewing safari, 111
  dog sledding, 113

Griffin, Bob, 70

Hathaway, Norm, 53

Hawaiian Islands trip, 138

Himalayan trek, 122

Honduras
  scuba trip, 130

Hunting
  Upland shooting, 88
  Water Fowl, 92
  Big Game, 95
  Firearms, 106

Hunting Trip, preparation, 105

Iceland
  fishing, 48
  viewing safari, 111

Insect bites, 84

Iran
  hunting, 101

Jacklin, Bob, 44

James Bay, 92

Jerstad, Lute, 122

Johann, Ed, 133

Jungle Queen, the, 121

Kayaking, 133

Kerbis, Don, 142
Kilbride, Bert and Jackie, 131
K Bar Z Ranch, 102

Les Menuires, 153
Lilly, Bud, 44
Little Dix Bay Hotel, 131

Miller, Paul J., 157
Micronesia
  scuba trip, 130
Mistassini Park, 42
Montana
  fly fishing, 43
  ranch, 140
Morocco
  golf, 149
Mountaineering
  See Climbing
Mozambique
  hunting, 96, 97

National Fish Stamp
  Program, 122
Nepal, 122
New Zealand
  fishing, 47
  hunting, 103

Observaion, 160
Outward Bound, 142
Open, the, 150

Panama, 56, 70
Paraguay, 71
Parismina Tarpon Rancho, 62
Perinchief, S.L. "Pete", 69
Peru, 116, 119
Pez Maya, 62
Pflueger Marine Taxidermy, 83
Photographer, the, 162-167
  travel procedures, 165
Photographic safaris, 110, 112
  115, 128
Plants (identification), 161
Pownall, Dick, 115
Pribilof Islands, 115
Punta Carnero, 58

Quetico-Superior canoe area, 135

Rafting, 133
Rakowitsch, Andre V., 121
Ramsay, Major Neil, 89
Reid, Douglas, 46
Roatan Island, 130
Royal Golf Club of Dar Es
  Salaam, 149

Safari
  hunting, 95, 96
  See also Photographic Safari
Sailing, 141, 142, 154-157
  schools, 156-157
Scotland
  fishing, 52
  golf, 150
  grouse, 89
Scuba
  instruction, 128
  travel specialists, 129
  trips, 129-131
Sea Pines Plantation
  tennis, 147
  sailing school, 157
Seamanship, 141, 156
Seasickness, 83
Skiing, 151-153
  travel with skis, 153
Ski touring (cross country), 139,
  142, 151
Sierra Nevada, 138
Snegamook Lake Lodge, 54
Snowbird, 151
Sotogrande, 148
South Africa, 110
South American archeological
  tour, 116
Spain
  golf, 148
  wingshooting, 90
Star Island Nautical Camp, 141
Sundance, 147
Survival skills, 142

Tallawahee Plantation, 88
Tennis, 142, 146-148
Tiger Hill Safari, 72

Travel Specialists, 129, 188
Tropic Star Lodge, 56
Tricomi, Jerry, 62
Tsalickis, Mike, 120
Turcotte, Lee and Helen, 130

Underwater exploration
  See Scuba

Vail Wilderness Backpacking, 132
Val Thorens, 153
Vieux Posts Lodge, 42
Viking Air Safaris, 111

Walker's Cay, 65
Wickenburg Inn, 146
"Wings in Iceland," 113
Woodstock Inn, 139
Wyoming
  hunting, 102
  family vacation, 136

Young people
  activities for, 140-142
  See also
  canoeing, 133
  climbing schools, 132
  fishing schools, 132
  sailing schools, 156
Yucatan, 62, 92

ACKNOWLEDGEMENTS

Written by *Mark J. Sosin*
Designed by *Norman Snyder Studios, Inc.*
Production supervised by *Frederick G. Mugler*
Editorial assistance from *Edith Rose Wilson*

Text set in Souvenir by *Expertype, Inc.,* New York City
Printed at *The Nimrod Press,* Boston
Covers by *Gilmore Leather Products, Inc.,* Andover, Mass.
Binding by *Publishers Binding Co.,* Winchester, Mass.

Published by *Richard E. Forrest*

With thanks to all those who worked on this book, and to
John Fry of Skiing magazine, Asher Birnbaum, Shepherd
Campbell and Cal Brown of Tennis and Golf Digest magazines,
Lou Garcia of Braniff International, Ed Murphy of Sports
Afield, Walt Hendrick, Tony Chiu, Slocum "Buz" Chapin of
Adventures Unlimited, and John W. Jenkins of Planaflex Company.

This book was made possible by the interest and support of
Harry G. Haskell, Jr., President, Alain Singer and Henry Geis,
Vice Presidents, and James S. Troy, Director of Special Projects,
all of Abercrombie & Fitch Co.

PHOTO CREDITS

Photographs were provided courtesy of: Swiss National Tourist Office, p.40; Mark J. Sosin, p.42, 45; Braniff International, p.46; Sosin, p.49, 52; Canadian National Tourist Bureau, p.54; Sosin, p.56, 58, 60, 62, 63, 64, 66, 67, 69, 71, 73; Norwegian National Travel Office, p.75; Ed Jaffee Studio, p.79; the Orvis Company, Inc., p.80; Sosin, p.84; Doug Knight Photo, p.88; Spanish National Tourist Office, p.90, 91; Adventures Unlimited, Inc., p.96, 98; Iranian Tourist Organization, Inc., p.101; New Zealand Consulate General, N.Y., p.104; Remington Arms Company, Inc., p.105; Royal Danish Ministry for Foreign Affairs, p.108; Sosin, p.110; Outdoors, Inc., p.112; Royal Danish Ministry for Foreign Affairs, p.113, 114; Braniff International, p.115, 116, 117, 118, 119, 120; Outdoors, Inc., p.121, 122; Nepalese Consulate General, p.123; American River Touring Association, p.126; Gene Tinker, p.128; Fred Brodersen, p.131; Dick Pownall, p.132; Joe Cole, Nantahala Outdoor Center, p.134; Wilderness Outfitters, p.135; Grand Teton Lodge Company, p.137; Continental Campers, Inc., p.138; Woodstock Ski Touring Center, p.139; Chase Ranch, p.140, 141; Outward Bound, Inc., 142; Princess Hotels, Inc., p.144; Sundance, p.146; Nyle Leatham, p.147; Robert E. Warner, Inc., p.148; Moroccan National Tourist Office, p.149; the Village at Bretton Woods, p.152; French Government Tourist Office, p.153; Columbia Yacht Corporation, p.154; Offshore Sailing School, p.157; Harold Martin, Nikon, p.158, 163 (bottom); R. Forrest, p.163 (top); Photo by Tobey, p.171; Trans World Airlines, p.174.